# Ava's Bedside

## Making Sense Through Attachment

Nobo Komagata
Sachiko Komagata

Lulu.com

Ava's Bedside: Making Sense Through Attachment
by Nobo Komagata and Sachiko Komagata

ISBN  978-1-4357-0731-3
Library of Congress Control Number:  2008900129


Published by
Lulu.com
860 Aviation Parkway, Suite 300
Morrisville, NC 27560
http://www.lulu.com

March 2008.

Printed in the United States of America.


Publication information:
http://lulu.com/phenomenologic
This title is also available for download.

Authors' contact:
e-mail: avasbedside@phenomenologic.com

To Anna,

For her third birthday

# Table of Contents

# Part 1: The Story

Once upon a time, there was a grandma hippo, called Ava, who became very ill. So she went to the best hippo hospital in the area, far away from her home. Unfortunately, she had a sense that she was going to stay there for a long time, possibly for the rest of her life.

Ava had two daughters. But neither of them visited her very often. Ava had several close friends as well. But none of them visited her very often either.

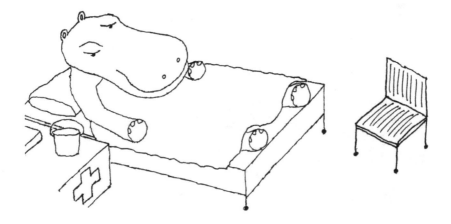

One day, her nurse hippo, Disa, came in and said, "Nobody visits you, huh?"

"That's none of your business!" Ava replied. "My daughters are very busy. In addition, our family motto is independence. I taught my daughters how to be independent by being a good example."

"Oh, no," Disa said. "I'm from a kind of broken family. I know how to be independent, I mean, real independent. My parents used to call me names, hit me, ignore me ..."

There was a long pause. Then, Disa swallowed a pill in front of Ava and continued. "Ugh! But somewhere in my mind, I still miss them. I know I will feel miserable, but I still want to visit them—maybe through the back door. Yes, it's a strange feeling. I fear *and* miss them at the same time, as my therapist tells me."

Disa showed an expression which Ava has never seen. The left half of her face was fearful, while the right half was nostalgic.

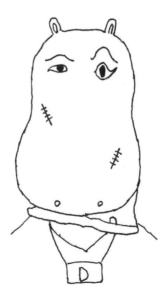

"No! It's completely different for me," said Ava. "I'm from a good family. I know my children feel the same. None of us are abusive or violent. I don't think you understand my situation."

"Don't you really wish your kids would visit you more often?" Disa persisted.

"No," Ava responded firmly. "We are just fine as we are. Leave me alone!"

Frankly, Ava was a little sympathetic to Disa, considering her difficult upbringing. But she was also humiliated by Disa's blunt manner. Something was disturbing Ava. She thought that she had a good life. When she was a child, she always got a lot of gifts from her parents and relatives. She traveled to many exotic places. She was good at school. Her marriage was all right. She also served as the chairperson of a community water management council. After her retirement, she gave a lot of her acquired "resources" to her daughters.[*]

---

[*] Even though hippos do not use "money" as we normally understand, they do employ various other means to do the same thing.

She thought she was perfectly fine, even if her relatives and friends did not visit her. But secretly, she started to wonder if that was really the case.

Ava also recalled the time when her mother was dying. *Of course, I supported her by providing resources when she was dying in this hospital. But actually, I didn't visit her very often. At that time, I was busy with my job at the council. Even when my mother finally passed away, I was thinking more about my job than about her. Well, that's normal for a hippo with a career, isn't it?*

The next day, her doctor hippo, Amba, came in and said, "Oh, my poor Ava. It's kind of dry in this area, isn't it? How are you doing?"

"Well, I'm fine," Ava replied, "Except for that talkative nurse. Will you ask her not to mind my business?"

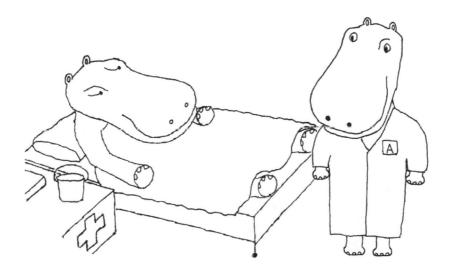

"Oh, you mean Disa?" Amba was aware. "I know, I know. She sometimes talks a bit too much. I do get mad at her comments sometimes. But she is not a bad hippo. Actually, she does all the nursing stuff pretty well, you know. What did she say to you?"

"Nothing serious," Ava tried to calm down. "Just a little bit about my family."

"Aha! That's what she is really good at," Amba sounded excited. "What is your problem? Did she say that you had few visitors? Did she tell you about her dead parents?"

"Dead? Crazy!" Ava was surprised. "No way can she understand my family situation! We are just fine. My daughters are very busy, you know."

"Oh, Ava! Why are you so stubborn?" said Amba. "If I were you, I would feel really, really lonely. When I was a kid, I desperately clung to my mom. She was always very kind ... well, sometimes. But she gets mad at small things very easily.* Things like kissing her ears, biting her tail, climbing on top of her ... Oh, no! Mom! I hate you."

---

* The mixed use of present and past tenses is intentional. See the commentary (p. 56) for an explanation.

Amba almost started to cry. But then, she seemed OK. "I'm sorry. I didn't know when Mom would be nice or upset. I always, always wanted my mom's love. You know, that's the only thing I wanted and still want."

"You remember small things quite well," commented Ava. "I don't."

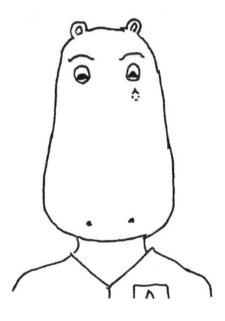

"Sorry, again," Amba said. "I am a cute little girl. I mean, I was. But why didn't my mom always love me? She probably loved me only when she wanted to do so, not really responding to my feelings. That's not what I'm doing with my child. Well, I'm trying.... But for some reason, my baby is very clingy. Often, I don't know what to do. Maybe she was born that way."

Amba told Ava many other things, including how her marriage is going.

After Amba left, Ava was even more disturbed. Disa and Amba are obviously very different. But they both miss their parents, even dead ones! She also felt that neither Disa nor Amba really understood her emerging, inner feelings.

The next day, a hippo called Seca came in to clean and said, "Lady, you look confused today. What's the matter?"

"Well, hippos here are rather rude," Ava started. "They probe and comment on my family issues."

"Lady, they must be trying to help you," said Seca.

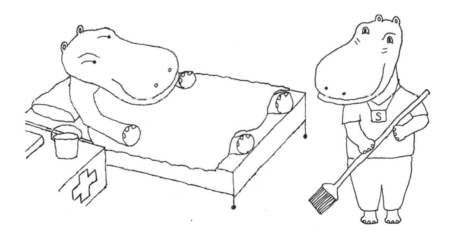

"Help me? Thank you very much!" Ava was surprised. "If they really want to help me, why can't they just leave me alone?"

"Lady, do you really want to be left alone?" Seca looked puzzled. "I don't think that is healthy. I am just a cleaning hippo and don't want to appear rude, like others. But if you want, I'd be happy to share my story with you."

"All right," said Ava. "You sound a bit different from the others."

"Lady, my family was very poor," Seca started her story.
"Actually, we are still poor. None of my family has
enough resources to stay in a hospital like this, even if
we get very sick."

Seca paused and looked at Ava. "I'm sorry, lady. I
didn't mean to talk about illness. You will be just fine
soon."

"That's all right," Ava said. "Please continue."

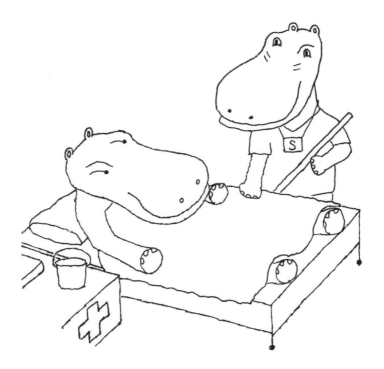

"Yes, lady," Seca continued. "My family members have been helping one another as long as I can remember. When my mom became seriously ill, we all took turns looking after her, at home. When she passed away, my dad was out of a job and I was out of school. If I had stayed in school, I would be a doctor now. Do I regret what I did? No, not at all! I have a beautiful memory of my mom. That helps me go on even during hard times. And, if I become ill, my daughters would do the same for me. We believe we can make sense of our lives that way. To make sense, we count on our ability to connect emotionally with others across time. I just know it because my parents always responded to my feelings."

Ava was stunned. Various thoughts came to her mind. *Why does this poor, old hippo sound so satisfied? Why am I not happier and not realizing that? Is it such a terrible thing that my relatives and friends do not visit me? Are they really thinking of me?*

Now, Ava tried to recall how she *really* lived her
childhood. For some reason, she could not do it very
well, unlike other hippos. She always thought that she
had a good childhood. But she could not fill in the
details. For example, she could not really remember
many details from all those exotic trips, or for that
matter, how she *really* felt about them.

Ava started to feel very uneasy. She wanted to talk with her parents. But they were long gone. She also wanted to talk with her daughters. But she did not know how to express her feelings. She even started to doubt if she could *feel* as other hippos do.

After days of thinking, Ava came to realize that her
childhood was filled with material things and other
"forms," but not with emotions or "meaning." She also
guessed that her daughters must have been in the same
situation. Now, it seemed clear. The lack of emotional
connections with other hippos, including her family and
friends, must be troubling her. She was able to cover it
up until she became ill. But now, she could no longer
hide her loneliness with other things.

Realizing what has been missing, Ava became desperate. She thought about a way to overcome it. But she was dying. She did not know how much time was left. She could never change her past. And, by now, almost all of her life was in the past. So, she felt that she had to give it all up.

Then, something happened to her. She was actually relieved. She had to accept her reality, although it was not a really satisfying one. Ava started to cry for a long time. This was the first time she cried for as long as she could remember. She did not cry even at her mother's funeral. It seemed that all of the blocked emotions were coming out of her.

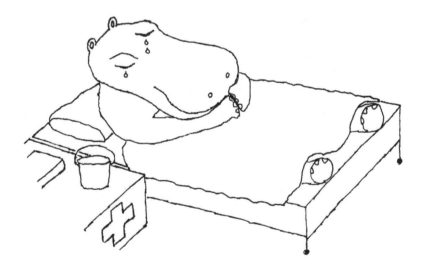

Ava wanted to talk with someone close, her daughters. Ava called one of them, Ida, and asked to visit her.

Approaching Ava's bed, Ida said, "You know, Mom. I'm very busy."

Ava started to cry. Ida was embarrassed but did not know what to say.

"Oh, Ida, I'm sorry..." said Ava. "I wish things had been different. But I cannot change the past. These days, I have been thinking about many things, especially things between you and me."

"Well, you are a great Mom," said Ida.

"No, no!" Ava stopped. "But remember? When you came in, you seemed almost angry at me. You sounded as though you sacrificed your valuable time for me."

"Don't analyze me, Mom," said Ida. "Yes, you are right. Things weren't right. Whenever I think about raising my daughter, I do it in a way different from my childhood. I just don't think you did it the right way. I don't want my daughter to repeat my experience."

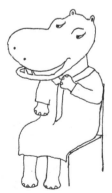

Before the visit, Ava wanted to communicate her
feelings with Ida. But this did not happen. Ava felt that
Ida was defensive and accusative. This was not new to
Ava. Ava has been that way too. But this time, Ava
was able to reflect upon the situation. Ava was actually
able to see herself in Ida. *She didn't express her feelings. I*
*didn't do that either. We were unable to communicate our*
*feelings. This is like the situation between my mom and me.*

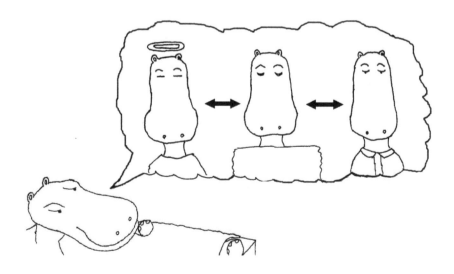

Several days passed. Ava was still suffering from the
confrontation with Ida. This was not the first time Ava
had such a conversation with Ida. However, this time,
Ava felt worse because she started to understand their
relationship problem and still could not repair it.

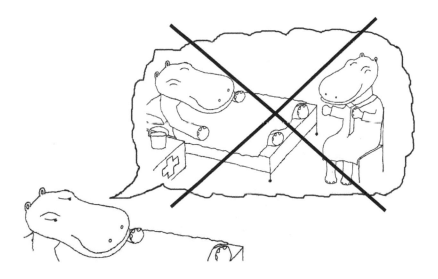

One day, Ava's other daughter, Dana, made a surprise
visit to her.

"Oh, my dear! What brought you here?" Ava asked.

"I don't know, Mom," replied Dana. "I just felt like
coming."

"Well, I have been thinking about many things these
days," said Ava. "I don't think I have been a good
mother."

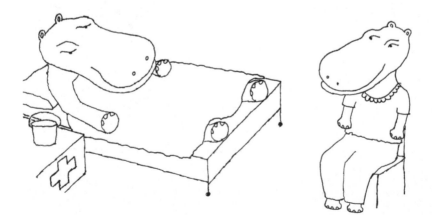

"What are you talking about?" said Dana. "You are a great mom."

"No, no," Ava stopped Dana. Ava wanted to avoid the same mistake she made with Ida. "I'm not talking about if it *looks* good. I'm talking about how you have been feeling. Other than today, did you feel like seeing me?"

"Well, not really," Dana appeared embarrassed. "I'm sorry, Mom. I have been very busy."

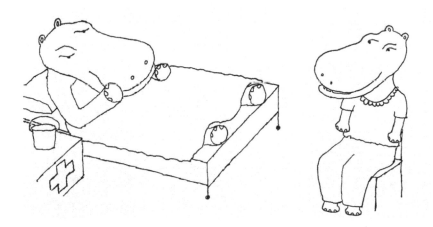

"I know," said Ava. "But is that the real reason? Honey, it's OK. Be honest. Now, I know that I would be feeling the same way if I were you. Recently, I thought about my relationship with my mother. I don't think my mother really understood and responded to my feelings. I probably had some feelings deep within me. But I grew up learning to suppress and not to express them. I am now convinced that you must be feeling the same way."

Dana was speechless.

That day, Ava and Dana talked about their feelings. To be precise, they talked more about a lack of feelings. It was the first time they openly discussed such a topic.

Ava did not have much time to live with her renewed
understanding of her relationships with other hippos.
But Ava felt that this short period of time seemed far
more meaningful than all of her past. In fact, to Ava,
this short period of time seemed almost eternal.


The End

# Part 2: Commentary

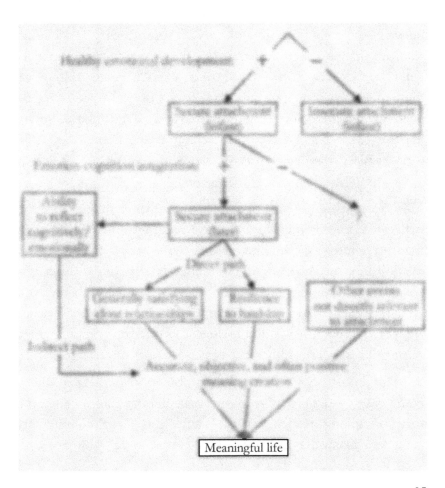

# Introduction

In the story, Ava thought that she had a good childhood, a lot of resources, and a prestigious job. However, toward the end of her life, she was still not really satisfied with her life. Rather, her life did not seem meaningful to her. In other words, she had trouble fully making sense of her life.[1] After her conversations with other hippos, Ava realized that the missing element was satisfying close relationships. To some people, or in this case, hippos, such as Seca, the connection between close relationships and a meaningful life seems obvious. Why, then, is it not obvious to others? What would be the principle underlying the connection between a meaningful life and close relationships? How could such a principle affect our lives? For those who share some traits with Ava, answers to these questions must be vital. However, these questions should be important for all of us, because nobody is completely free from relationship issues. Even those who are like Seca, as well as Disa and Amba, may well experience eventful relationships.

In this commentary, we explore "attachment theory" as one of the most important principles underlying the connection between a meaningful life and close relationships. Attachment theory points to the importance of early child-caregiver relationships in the rest of one's life; it also underscores the ability of adults to reflect upon their relationships and lives. Understanding the ideas in attachment theory and related fields, we could strengthen and broaden our insight into our own relationships and possibly make better sense of our lives.

This book is organized as a combination of a fable and a commentary. This way, we hope that at least the fable can be read by young readers; at the same time, the commentary provides an in-depth discussion of the fable with research information in a readable form. Due to the nature of the topics, the commentary is fairly complex. However, we have tried to make it self-contained.

Before proceeding, some qualifications are in order. First, although attachment theory must be one of the most important factors involved in making sense of one's life, it is just one of many. Our lives are really complex events, and it would be impossible to make full sense of them without considering all of the involved factors, which is way beyond the scope of this book.

Next, the main purpose of this commentary is to provide a readable and meaningful background to the story. Often, we make our own interpretations in order to make this commentary appropriate for our purposes, although we try to be as accurate as possible with respect to the current state of the field. So, the reader should expect this to be a narrative for making sense rather than scientific prose.

The main source of the information is two books on attachment theory: one by Robert Karen and the other by Daniel Siegel. Both of them are highly recommended. Karen has details on the development of attachment theory.[2] Siegel includes a concise description of attachment theory in connection to emotion and memory in the context of complex systems.[3] We also rely on a handbook edited by Jude Cassidy and Phillip Shaver, a collection of articles through the late 1990s[4] and some more recent work relevant to attachment theory.[5] Some other references will be cited later. Finally, we note that attachment theory is not the same thing as attachment parenting or bonding. We will come back to this point later in the Parenting section.

## Meaningful Life and Close Relationships

A meaningful life is not possible without satisfying close relationships. Obviously, this premise is reflected in the story. Ava started to doubt whether she had a meaningful life only after becoming terminally ill and through conversations with other hippos. Although it is not clear whether Ava was *really* able to overcome her problem, it would be better to be able to make *some* sense than no sense at all. This naturally contrasts with Seca, who appears to have a meaningful life with satisfying close relationships.

Many people would accept this premise as it is seen in the story and also in literature, for example, "A Christmas Carol." Many non-human animals rely on social instincts as well, as can be seen in the cover picture of this book: a mother-child pair of giraffes, a flock of birds, and a swarm of ants. For those who reject the premise, a question might be whether they could make sense of their lives at the moment of *their* deaths without satisfying relationships. Would they be satisfied with a lot of money, superior status, or unparalleled achievements? One might also recall the film "Citizen Kane." In the film, a media tycoon dies with the last word, "Rosebud." A reporter searches for the meaning of the word, hoping to write a glamorous story. As the reporter fails to find the meaning of the word, the film ends with a scene showing a sled, on which the word is written. It is the sled he was riding when he was separated from his mother. The last scene articulates the importance of meaningful relationships. Despite the naturalness of the premise, it is still just a premise and cannot be "proven" or "refuted." In the rest of this section, we briefly explore some ideas underlying the premise from a few different but related perspectives. We will return to this premise in a later section (Attachment and

Meaningful Life, p. 84), after more discussion of attachment theory.

One of the main elements connecting meaningfulness and close relationships is emotion. Close relationships are the source of various feelings such as comfort and happiness, and even frustration and anger. When we can readily accept such emotions in an objective, hopefully positive way, we can make sense of the relationships and consequently, our lives. Thus, for a meaningful life, healthy emotional development is essential.[6] Although the importance of emotion is underestimated by many people, including scientists, emotions appear to be underlying almost all of our important mental activities and behaviors.[7]

However, emotions are particularly elusive, even compared to cognitive properties such as memory and vision. We are not even aware of much of our emotional activities, which may be unconscious. One aspect of the difficulty with emotions is that emotions are often associated with implicit memory.[8] In contrast to explicit memory, such as names and phone numbers, implicit memory cannot be recalled at will. However, implicit memory plays an important role in all arenas of our lives. Implicit memory includes various emotions associated with a specific animal, person, or situation, which are activated without explicit effort to *recall* the association between the stimulus and the response. An important point about the difference between these two types of memory is that explicit memory does not develop until around the age of eighteen months. Thus, the only type of memory available to infants is implicit. It is during infanthood that emotions start to develop, without any recollection. It has also been documented that early implicit memory affects behavior throughout one's life, as will be discussed in later sections.

This clearly suggests the following. Our behaviors, including those involved in close relationships, are partly based on our implicit memory, which begins formation in infanthood, and to which we do not have direct access. Thus, in order to understand the connection between meaningful life and close relationships, we need to know our early relationships and emotional development.

This is where attachment theory can offer a great deal. One of the implications of attachment theory is that how one deals with various close relationships would be affected by her* earliest relationships. Furthermore, it is often the case that people with attachment issues would not realize the problems caused by them, because it derives from early relationships experienced before the development of explicit memory.

## Attachment Theory

Attachment theory, as it is commonly referred to, was pioneered by John Bowlby and Mary Ainsworth.[9] The main points of the theory, as we understand them, are: (1) infants have an innate desire to form an affectional tie, referred to as "attachment," with a small number of caregivers; (2) attachment is a developmental process which forms during the first few years of life but continues to develop throughout life; and (3) the attachment is a part of an integrated process for the individual, also including exploration and caregiving. While these might sound more or less commonsensical to some people, these ideas were developed in a context where other less commonsensical theories were

---

* We tend to use the *grammatical* female gender referring to a person in a *biologically* neutral manner due to the lack of an appropriate neutral pronoun in English. Such a use may be justified because, developmentally speaking, the default biological gender is female.

dominant.    It should also be pointed out that various consequences and implications of the above-mentioned points are very important for making sense of our lives.  In this section, we discuss the basics of attachment theory as well as some background on the development of the theory.

Considering the vulnerability of human babies, the ability to be taken care of must be the very first and most important quality of a baby.  Then, it is not surprising that a human baby is born with a desire to form attachment to a few caregivers who are expected to protect her.    This assumption has strong implications.    The result of violation of the basic need for attachment can be seen in many cases of institutional maternal deprivation, for example, in Romanian orphanages.[10]    These children may never be able to be close to other people.  The consequence is possibly irreversible.  While this assumption emphasizes the innate aspect of attachment, it also underscores the impact of child rearing.  This is because attachment formation is contingent upon the availability and the quality of caregivers. In this regard, attachment theory has a realistic view about how nature and nurture interact, unlike extremes such as nativism and "tabula rasa" (or "blank slate").

As long as a baby is cared for by a small number of main caregivers, she will form attachment with the caregivers by the end of the first year (although the quality of the attachment will vary depending on the situation).  However, the attachment with the caregivers will continue to develop after that period.  Her attachment patterns will also be affected by different types of later close relationships.    At the same time, later close relationships would also be affected by earlier attachment.  The assumption that attachment is a developmental process is an important one.  The need for attachment security may well be the number one human desire, even across the life span.  As such, attachment problems even after the first few years of life would be crucial for our lives. We will discuss later how attachment patterns might continue and change. Although it is not as critical as in some other animals, such as geese, it seems that there is a sensitive period for forming attachment.

When we discuss attachment, we actually need to be more specific about three related aspects: attachment, exploration, and caregiving.[11] Attachment behaviors are to seek proximity to a caregiver (by grasping, clinging, reaching, or crawling), cry, vocalize, and smile (e.g., as approaching a caregiver). These behaviors are in general activated when an infant (or any person, really) is frightened, distressed, ill, or tired. In this case, the attachment figure functions as the "safe haven." Exploration behaviors are to play, discover new environments, and interact with peers. Strictly speaking, these behaviors occur only when the attachment needs are satisfied. In this case, the attachment figure functions as the "secure base." We all need to explore for various reasons and also to feel safe and secure through attachment behaviors, although we may not realize such needs later in our lives. Thus, the balance between attachment and exploration behaviors is extremely important, much like the use of the accelerator and brake when driving a car.[12] This attachment-exploration balance can also be seen as intimacy-independence balance and is closely related to the distinction between negative and positive emotions.[13] In contrast, caregiving behaviors are to provide a safe haven (for proximity seeking) and a secure base (for exploration) for another person attached to the caregiver.

How would most individuals develop the innate attachment desire into balanced attachment and exploration behaviors? This question has been answered by Bowlby through the idea of the "internal working model" (IWM).[14] That is, an infant begins to *internalize* the interaction with her caregivers as a basis for the interactions involved in all later close relationships. The mechanism is considered as a *working* model because it will be continuously modified throughout the person's life. This is roughly how infant attachment affects later close relationships. Not just attachment, but other aspects of early emotional development can also affect one's life tremendously.[15] Then, it is not surprising that there are a variety of psychological and social consequences of early emotional development.[16] Bowlby was specific about the impact of child rearing for later psychological well-being, studying the behaviors of many war orphans after World War II. Furthermore, since the earliest memories are implicit (and thus cannot be recalled explicitly), we cannot normally realize how our earliest experience affects our close relationships and our lives in general. Even though attachment is only one fairly narrow aspect of life, it is nevertheless an extremely important one and relevant to many aspects of our lives.

Although Bowlby's idea may appear very reasonable nowadays, we need to understand a completely different environment where attachment theory was being developed. More specifically, attachment theory has been contrasted primarily with the Freudian psychoanalytic tradition of that time. Attachment theory shares with the psychoanalytic tradition the importance of unconscious parts of the mind. However, attachment theory emphasizes the importance of *real* relationships, including upbringing and interactions with parents[*] rather than fantasy.[17] Also unlike some aspects of psychoanalytic tradition, attachment theory does not single out the importance

---

[*] Although the child-caregiver attachment can form between an infant and any adult, including a non-parent, we often use the term "parent" to refer to the caregiver.

of breast feeding.[18]    Attachment theory also contrasts with behaviorism.  While behaviorists might characterize attachment simply as a sign of dependence, attachment theory emphasizes the balance between attachment and exploration as part of healthy development.[19]   In essence, attachment theory can be characterized by its emphasis on emotional/relational, realistic, and evolutionary/survival aspects.

While Bowlby focuses on the normative aspects, attachment theory discusses individual differences as well.  In this respect, the strength of attachment theory is also due to Ainsworth and colleagues' effort to devise a procedure to identify four different infant attachment patterns (described in the next section).  These attachment patterns can be identified mainly by observing how well a parent responds to the infant's needs.  However, since the parent's response is actually affected by the infant's behavior, it is more accurate to view the child-parent interaction as co-regulation, mutual regulation, or attuned communication/affect attunement.[20]

## Attachment Patterns

Ainsworth and her colleagues' careful observation of infants identified four different attachment patterns: secure, avoidant, ambivalent, and disorganized, as summarized in Table 1 (p. 45). In the following, we will use the table to look into the infant period of the four hippos in the story.

Ava is the character who had avoidant attachment.[*]   Note that all the characters in the story are named after the four attachment patterns.  For example, Ava is for "**av**oidant" with the

---

[*] To the authors' knowledge, the attachment patterns of hippopotamuses have never been researched.  The reader is asked to anthropomorphize them.

## Table 1: Attachment Patterns (Infant)

| | Attachment Patterns | | | |
|---|---|---|---|---|
| | | Insecure | | |
| | **Secure** | **Avoidant** | **Ambivalent** or Resistant | **Disorganized** or Disoriented |
| | | Organized | | |
| When with parent (with little distress) | Explores actively | Explores actively | Little exploration, preoccupied with parent, clingy | May show fear, freezing, contradictory behaviors |
| When in distress (e.g., separation from parent) | Cries | Does not cry | Cries | *May fit in one of the organized patterns (left)* |
| Upon reunion with parent | Seek proximity, quickly soothed, resumes exploration | Avoids/ignores parent, focuses on toys | Continues to cry, fails to settle *and* explore | |
| Parent characteristics | Emotionally available | Rejecting, intrusive, controlling | Inconsistent | Abusive, threatening |
| | | Good enough | | Problematic |
| Distribution[i] | 60% | 20% | 10% | 10% |

[i] These are hypothetical numbers based on *our* reading of the literature. Furthermore, the disorganized classification is usually given in addition to some organized classification; thus, the percentage figures in the literature do not necessarily sum up to 100%.

"-**a**" suffix, commonly used for a female name. Analogously, Disa, Amba, and Seca are supposed to have had **dis**organized, **amb**ivalent, and **sec**ure attachment patterns, respectively.

Although we classify Ava, an adult, with respect to the attachment pattern in Table 1, these patterns are actually characterizations of infants. Thus, strictly speaking, Ava would have been classified as avoidant *when she was an infant*. For the sake of the discussion in this section, we assume that infant attachment patterns continue throughout life (more on this point in later sections). Looking at Table 1, we can guess how Ava would have behaved. For example, with her parent, she would have explored the environment actively, would not have cried even if she was in moderate distress (e.g., her parent leaving the scene), and would have even avoided/ignored the parent on return. This is a consequence of parenting, which is most likely rejecting, intrusive, and/or controlling.

On the other hand, a secure infant, such as Seca, would have cried when her parent left the scene but would have sought proximity and been soothed quickly upon reunion. The main source of secure attachment is emotional availability of the parent. This is probably an oversimplified description, and thus calls for more explanation. Especially during the first few years of Seca's life, her parents must have been available to her (probably most of the time), observed Seca very attentively, felt Seca's facial and bodily expression, and responded to Seca's needs in a timely and comforting manner. Her parent would be accepting, understanding, attending, consistent, and never be abusive or threatening. She would know Seca's various needs, such as hunger, thirst, and elimination, and would attend to frustration and fear. She would not force certain things just because of her convenience. To some people, this type of response might appear to be overindulgent. However, during the first year, there is no such thing as overindulgence. On the other hand, when Seca was a toddler, her parent may have given her more structure. Her parent might have taught Seca how to regulate herself and how to behave morally in a confident and consistent manner. Still, the parent must have done this based on secure attachment, i.e., first addressing and accepting Seca's needs.

An infant with ambivalent attachment, such as Amba, would have been clingy, would not have explored much, and would have tended to cry a lot. Her behaviors can be characterized as a combination of seeking intimacy and expressing hostility toward her parents.[21] This is mainly due to the inconsistent behavior of her parents. They may have attended to Amba in a warm manner at some times but rejected her in other times. People like Amba would, as a result, become hungry for parental response.

An infant with disorganized attachment, such as Disa, would have manifested the conflicting behaviors of being attracted to a parent (except for extreme cases) and trying to escape from the same parent. This is because the parent is both the attachment figure and the source of threat. Disorganized infants may also attempt to take control over the parent.[22] Furthermore, people with disorganized attachment have a high risk of psychological problems. In the story, Disa mentions seeing a therapist and takes medication.

The finding that infants can be classified into these four patterns opens a way to discuss attachment from various perspectives. The patterns are important for discussing how an infant begins to internalize close relationships in her specific environment. With longitudinal studies, we can learn how early attachment affects one's later life. Since the earliest memories are implicit and cannot be recalled, knowing one's infant attachment pattern could tell her what was really going on when she was growing up. We will return in later sections to the topic of how we could tell our infant attachments without knowing our past.

Since attachment patterns are such an important concept and yet are rather difficult to grasp, we discuss some relevant points about the patterns. For example, the behavior of an avoidant infant would appear very independent, and thus may appear desirable, especially in Western culture. However, it is actually a sign of insecure attachment. As will be discussed below, insecure attachment is not necessarily a bad thing. However, there are certain consequences, for example, difficulty with both close relationships and making sense of their lives. Suppose that a parent trains an infant not to cry even when she is in distress, or leaves her to "cry it out," that is, to cry without responding to her. Then, the parent is promoting avoidant attachment. If an infant is securely attached to her parent, she would cry upon separation (distress for most infants), which might appear timid to some people. Nevertheless, the infant can grow *healthy* dependence, which will be important for attachment continuity (again, more in later sections).

Although disorganized attachment is considered problematic, the other three patterns are considered within the normal range and adaptive to relevant environments. They are also considered as a result of "good enough" parenting.[23] In fact, there must be a niche for avoidant and ambivalent people.[24] For example, in modern society, many jobs can be performed well without good relationship skills. In certain workplaces, socialization is strongly discouraged. On the other hand, certain artistic professions may be better performed with emotional bursts rather than stability. However, secure children tend to possess more "desirable" properties, for example, being popular in school settings.[25] Secure attachment is thus associated with better quality of life.[26]

When multiple caregivers are available, different attachment patterns can be observed for different caregivers. For example, infants can be securely attached to the mother while avoidantly attached to the father. This is because an attachment pattern is a consequence of child-parent co-regulation, and the interaction is unique to each pair. Infants normally organize such multiple attachment patterns in a hierarchical manner. For example, if an infant is mainly taken care of by her mother, the attachment to her mother would naturally be the strongest. Furthermore, mixed attachment patterns may be associated with certain specific contexts.[27] That is, even with a single caregiver, different patterns may be observed, for example, at home and outside the home.

Attachment patterns are mainly due to the balance between attachment and exploration behaviors. Each of these behavioral systems is already very complex, involving various factors including temperament and culture. Thus, there is always a possibility of those factors affecting the patterns. We will discuss the impact of temperament in a later section (Critical Discussion of Attachment Theory, p. 57). As for culture, the distribution of attachment patterns is, in general, similar across cultures.[28] However, there are reports of substantially different distributions, for example, more prevalent attachment insecurity in Kibbutzim in Israel and some parts of Germany.[29] For the former, it may be due to the collective child rearing; for the latter, it appears to be due to the community's strong emphasis on independence from early years.

## Strange Situation

Infant attachment patterns are most commonly identified by a well-designed laboratory procedure called the "Strange Situation."[30] The main idea of the procedure is to induce moderate distress so that both attachment and exploration behaviors can be observed. To do this, the procedure more or less models a hospital waiting room with attractive toys, where the parent of the infant leaves the room and a stranger joins the company at varying times. The procedure contains increasing levels of distress so that exploration and attachment behaviors at various levels can be observed. The actual sequence of this procedure is shown in Table 2 (p. 50).

Once we understand the basics of the attachment patterns as in Table 1, it is possible to predict the response of an infant. As

## Table 2: Strange Situation

| Episode | Key events | Child | Parent | Stranger |
|---------|-----------|-------|--------|----------|
| 1 | | Introduced | Introduced | *n/a* |
| 2 | | | | |
| 3 | | | *present* | Introduced<br>Plays with child |
| 4 | First separation | | Leaves | *present* |
| 5 | First reunion | *present* | Returns | *present*<br>Leaves quietly |
| 6 | Second separation | | Leaves | *n/a* |
| 7 | | | *n/a* | Enters |
| 8 | Second reunion | | Returns | *present*<br>Leaves quietly |

long as the parent is present in the room, a secure infant would explore the environment, where there are a lot of attractive toys. When her parent leaves, the infant would protest and cry (attachment behaviors). Upon her parent's return, the infant would greet the parent and quickly be soothed (attachment behaviors), and then return to play (exploration). The balance between attachment and exploration behaviors is quite natural.

An avoidant infant would explore the room like a secure infant. However, she may not cry when her parent leaves and may even ignore the return of the parent. That is, her normal exploration behaviors are matched by minimal attachment behaviors. An ambivalent infant would be clingy (attachment behavior) throughout the procedure and not explore much. A disorganized infant would exhibit behaviors such as some combination of approaching to and escaping from the parent, as described in the previous section.

The procedure is normally applied to infants at the age of 12 months, possibly as old as 18 months, but before substantial development of speech and other cognitive skills. After this period, the level of distress induced in the Strange Situation may become too different among children. For example, some children would be very accustomed to separation from parents.[31] Furthermore, the procedure would have increasingly different meanings depending on cultures.

Due to the ingenious design, the Strange Situation is considered fairly robust. However, there are still some potential issues. For example, the procedure may not be as accurate for identifying attachment patterns with a father.[32] This may be because fathers tend to encourage exploration more than mothers.

## Attachment Continuity

One of the main theses of attachment theory is that infant attachment patterns could predict certain behaviors of the person at later stages of her life, if no other significant impacts appear later in life. This qualification is important. Some opponents of attachment theory mistakenly argue that attachment theory proposes a kind of determinism (see Critical Discussion of Attachment Theory, p. 57). Bowlby and his colleagues explicitly reject such an idea. The richness of life makes it possible to overcome disadvantages in one's early life, or the other way around. Nevertheless, it is striking that attachment continuity in general has been demonstrated by research.[33] In many cases, it may be due to the consistency of the child-parent interaction across the life span of the child. That is, even though the behavior of the child changes as she grows, the parents' response and other environmental factors may support continuity.

Attachment continuity can be seen in two ways: *intra-* and *inter-*generation, i.e., within a single generation (person) and across multiple generations, respectively. In the previous paragraph, we discussed the former. The latter aspect can be seen in how the attachment patterns of parents affect their children. It turns out that the attachment patterns of parents are the best predictor of the attachment patterns of their children.[34] Again, since so many factors are involved, it is not at all deterministic.

In the story, Ava's children, Ida and Dana, are also supposed to have avoidant attachment (these names are from the middle of the word "avoidant" with the "-a" suffix for female names). Ava's mother is also supposed to be avoidant. On the other hand, Seca's family is likely to consist of mainly securely attached people. Disa's family would experience disorganized attachment through generations. Abused children are more likely to become abusive themselves.[35] Once again, these possibilities are not at all deterministic due to various factors in life.

Then, did Ava change from avoidant to secure attachment at the end of the story? Not very likely. If the attachment pattern changes, it is not likely to occur in a short period of time. It would also require substantial experience. So, for many people, even after realizing one's own insecure attachment, it would not go away so easily, especially later in life. However, for some people, just realizing their own attachment patterns would be a life-changing event. For example, Dana might have realized this after her discussion with Ava. If Dana has a chance to raise a child, she may be able to change her behavior and may be able to have secure attachment with her child. But this must be a challenge. Let us recall that attachment pattern forms during the first few years of life, when only implicit memory is available. Unless one makes an effort to learn her own attachment by carefully studying attachment theory, she may never really know what her attachment pattern is. That is, it is highly possible that one lives with no idea about one of her deepest behavior patterns.

However, in some cases, attachment patterns can change. For example, people with insecure (infant) attachment pattern may turn out to be like securely attached people, an occurrence referred to as "earned secure" attachment.[36] In such a case, it is most likely that certain positive close relationships, for example, with some adult mentor, may have changed the attachment pattern. However, once a child develops insecure attachment with her parents, it would be a challenge to develop secure attachment with someone else due to the learned way of dealing with close relationships.[37]

There are many potential problems with discussing attachment continuity. One is the status of adult attachment. Earlier, we noted that an infant may have multiple distinct attachment patterns associated with different caregivers. Then, how would the two parents' different attachment patterns affect the children? The current understanding in the field is that when a child becomes an adult, she integrates multiple, possibly different, attachment patterns into a single attachment pattern.[38] This process most likely takes place during adolescence. In general, the attachment pattern with the strongest attachment figure, for example, the mother, would be the basis for one's adult attachment pattern.

Another problem with analyzing attachment continuity *was* the lack of a procedure to identify adult attachment patterns. A breakthrough was made by Mary Main, a student of Mary Ainsworth, and her colleagues; the procedure is called "Adult Attachment Interview" (AAI).

## Adult Attachment Interview (AAI)

This procedure consists of a semi-formatted interview about the subject's childhood with an extensive analysis of the narrative.[39]

Types of questions used in the interview are shown in Table 3 (p. 55).[40]

The development of AAI was a really innovative idea. The AAI analyzes not only the content of the narrative but also its delivery. The applicability of such an analysis comes from the connection between mental organization during the first years and mental activities throughout one's life.[41] In particular, AAI applies principles in linguistic pragmatics proposed by Paul Grice, called Maxims of Conversation.[42] The main points of the principle include the following. When people are engaged in a conversation, they are supposed to cooperate in a way that their contribution is optimal with respect to truthfulness, amount of information, relevance, and clarity. If one violates any one of these, one is actually trying to convey some hidden meaning not explicit in the message. People with secure attachment tend to be able to follow Maxims of Conversation well, through internalization of their early relationships with their parents. On the other hand, people with insecure attachment tend to violate Maxims of Conversation, even when they are not trying to convey hidden meaning. For example, preoccupied/ambivalent people tend to be too long while dismissing/avoidant people tend to be too brief in their comments.

Note that these characteristics are not always present. They are activated especially when people are engaged in or reflecting upon close relationships, for example, during an AAI about their parents. Thus, it is inappropriate to extend this type of interpretation to other forms of written and spoken expressions. Although our story is not an AAI, it is written in a way that the hippos discuss their relationships and childhoods. So, some of the properties used in AAI analysis can still be observed. Analysis of adult attachment using the narrative obtained during an AAI session is shown in Table 4 (p. 56). The most important

## Table 3:  Adult Attachment Interview Questions

1. To begin with, could you just help me to get a little bit oriented to your family–for example, who was in your immediate family, and where you lived?
2. Now I'd like you to try to describe your relationship with your parents as a young child, starting as far back as you can remember.
3. Could you give me five adjectives or phrases to describe your relationship with your **mother** during childhood?  I'll write them down, and when we have all five I'll ask you to tell me what memories or experiences led you to choose each one.
4. Could you give me five adjectives or phrases to describe your relationship with your **father** during childhood?  I'll write them down, and when we have all five I'll ask you to tell me what memories or experiences led you to choose each one.
5. To which parent did you feel closer, and why?
6. When you were upset as a child, what did you do, and what would happen?  Could you give me some specific incidents when you were upset emotionally?  Physically hurt?  Ill?
7. Could you describe your first separation from your parents?
8. Did you ever feel rejected as a child?  What did you do, and do you think your parents realized that they were rejecting you?
9. Were your parents ever threatening toward you–for discipline, or jokingly?
10. How do you think your overall early experiences have affected your adult personality?  Are there any aspects you consider a setback to your development?
11. Why do you think your parents behaved as they did during your childhood?
12. Were there other adults who were close to you–like parents–as a child?
13. Did you experience the loss of a parent or other close loved one as a child, or in adulthood?
14. Were there many changes in your relationship with parents between childhood and adulthood?
15. What is your relationship with your parents like for you currently?

point is that AAI classification matches Strange Situation classification very well.[43]

In the story, Ava (avoidant/dismissing) shows a few characteristics consistent with the dismissing pattern.  When she discusses her childhood, she refers to it as good, without providing evidence.  In general, she is brief when she talks about

## Table 4:  Adult Attachment Patterns

| | AAI classification | | | |
|---|---|---|---|---|
| | **Secure** or Autonomous | **Dismissing** | **Preoccupied** | **Disorganized** or Unresolved |
| | Corresponding Strange Situation classification | | | |
| | Secure | Avoidant | Ambivalent | Disorganized |
| Content | Objective (not idealizing), balanced, integrates self over time | Overgeneralizes, lacks evidence, not remembering, dismissing relationships | Preoccupied with past, blurring past/present/future | False belief (e.g., about deceased person), unresolved loss, contradictory |
| Delivery | Reasonably detailed, coherent, consistent | Excessively brief, inconsistent | Excessively long, overly emotional | Fearful, cries, prolonged pauses, incomplete sentences |
| Impact on personality | Balanced | Analytical, bullying | Emotionally unstable | Pathological |

her childhood.  Furthermore, she does not remember her childhood well.  Other dismissing responses include: "nothing" and "I don't know."[44]  Some of the characteristics can also be observed in Ida and Dana.  In general, an infant with avoidant Strange Situation classification would grow to be an adult with dismissing AAI classification.  In turn, she is most likely to raise children with avoidant attachment.  Since the root of the dismissing attachment pattern is the avoidant pattern in infancy, avoidant/dismissing people like Ava won't be aware of the cause of her attachment-related issues.

In contrast, Amba (ambivalent/preoccupied) easily gets very emotional.  Her comments are generally longer.  She also mixes up the grammatical tense, i.e., past and present.  The narrative of Seca (secure) is more balanced and coherent.  She can refer to her childhood objectively.  Although not listed in the table, her empathetic conversation style is not possible without fully conforming to Grice's Maxims of Conversation. Finally, Disa (disorganized) demonstrates certain characteristics of her attachment pattern, for example, pauses and incomplete sentences. Probably the most striking aspect is her false belief, which was told in a matter-of-fact manner: Disa talks about her dead parents as if they were alive.

## Critical Discussion of Attachment Theory

Attachment theory has evolved and developed during the past several decades. Despite the complexity associated with the ideas and measurement, research generates a lot of important results relevant to diverse areas, including parenting and romantic relationships. Nevertheless, there surely are people who argue against attachment theory on various points. One group would argue for genetic determinism, discounting the importance of the parenting process.[45] Another identifies peer influence as the primary source of child development.[46] Still another would emphasize the role of temperament and plasticity (these are somewhat contradictory, though) more so than attachment continuity.[47]

However, each of these arguments has been challenged. First, genetic influence on attachment pattern has been rejected relatively recently.[48] Attachment theory researchers' position is neither deterministic nor entirely environmental.[49] Nowadays, we know that the question is no longer about nature vs. nurture, but about how they interact.[50] Although nobody would deny the existence of peer influence, the impacts of one's parent on her peer choice has also been identified.[51] As for plasticity, we have already noted that attachment theory does not exclude the possibility. The attempt to explain attachment solely in terms of temperament has also been questioned.[52] One reason is that one can form multiple attachment patterns to different caregivers. This point can also be used against the argument for the genetic origin of attachment.

There also is a slightly different point made by Ed Tronick.[53] That is, attachment theory is bound to a specific set of cultures (in the "developed" world) and not applicable to some others. Since this is an intricate point, we discuss two examples used for this argument. The first case is about the Efé who live in the northeastern part of the Democratic Republic of Congo (formerly Zaire). According to Tronick, the Efé infants are cared for by a group of people. Efé mothers hold their babies much less than their Western counterpart. The babies are tossed around among many caregivers, as many as a dozen non-mothers a day. As a result, the babies appear to form attachments to many people, yet the attachments appear to be healthy. Tronick points out that this type of group care arrangement discounts the need for continuous care by a *small* number of caregivers, often considered as a strong implication of attachment theory. So, at least on one account, the attachment theory may be too strict; an infant must be able to develop attachment to more than a small number of caregivers. The second case is about the Kisii (or Gusii) who live in western Kenya. The Kisii mothers and infants are reported to have much less face-to-face interaction. Face-to-face interaction is considered essential for emotional development in the Western culture and also underlies attachment theory. Tronick argues that the Kisii example goes beyond what attachment theory can explain.

Contrary to Tronick's argument, we believe that attachment theory is actually useful to explain even the above-mentioned cases. First, Tronick's report on Efé includes some hints. The Efé approach appears to be a way to help mothers to balance child care and work within the available resources and is not really a "group" care, as observed in Kibbutzim (see p. 49).[54] Mothers sleep with their babies and caregivers are arranged around the mothers. In fact, when other people cannot console a baby, the baby's mother is called for. This strongly suggests the existence of attachment hierarchy. In this respect, the Efé child care arrangement is not fundamentally different from the arrangements of extended families with a lot of relatives living nearby. Furthermore, there is nothing wrong with the fact that an infant develops multiple positive attachments to others. Thus, as long as we do not limit the number of attachment figures to a small number, this case does not seem to be contrary to attachment theory.

Second, the case of Kisii is not necessarily a problem with attachment theory either. According to the information in Tronick's book, it is not clear what kind of attachment Kisii adults develop. If they tend to develop insecure attachment more so than Western cultures, it is possible that insecure attachment is promoted through the culture, much like the German case discussed earlier (p. 49). On the other hand, if the Kisii still develop secure attachments despite the lower degree of face-to-face interaction, co-regulation may be achieved through modes other than face-to-face interaction. It would not be surprising if blind infants developed secure attachment through non-facial interactions, although we are not aware of relevant data. In addition, we also question the methodology of the Kisii study. The data were gathered while Kisii infants were placed in a car seat (produced in the U.S.) and their mothers were instructed to "interact" with the infants. Such a procedure might be quite unnatural for their culture.

Many of the counter-arguments to attachment theory appear to be based on insufficient understanding of attachment theory.[55]

One of the most telling points is that some of the most prominent proponents of attachment theory, such as Alan Sroufe and Jay Belsky, were initially either outside of or critical about attachment theory in general and/or the Strange Situation in particular. They accepted ideas in attachment theory only after careful analysis.[56] Thus, it seems that the ideas in attachment theory are quite robust.

## Mechanisms Underlying Attachment

Many aspects of attachment theory are consistent with recent advancements in neuroscience.[57] Thus, it is possible to explain certain aspects of attachment theory using a developmental model mainly based on Daniel Siegel connecting the brain, emotions, memory, language, etc., which is summarized in Table 5 (p. 61). Note that the timing of each entry should not be taken too seriously. For example, linguistic development is very different among children.

The idea behind the present discussion is the notion of the internal working model (IWM). That is, during the first few years of life, we construct some sort of mental representation based on interaction with our caregivers.[58] The following subsections discuss certain anatomical areas, which are depicted in Figure 1 (p. 62) in an extremely simplified manner.

### *First Year: Emotional Development*

First, we briefly go through the developmental model and discuss certain points relevant to attachment. Already at birth, infants are social and emotional beings, at least in a primitive way. The architecture to be a social being further develops soon after birth. This includes the anterior cingulate cortex (ACC) for various

## Table 5: Developmental Model

| | Approximate age (years) | | |
|---|---|---|---|
| | 0 | 1 | 2 |
| Brain | Limbic system (parts) "Smart" vagus nerve Anterior cingulate cortex | Hippocampus, Prefrontal cortex | Corpus callosum |
| Emotion | Primary | Categorical/Basic | |
| Memory | Implicit (procedural, emotional) | Explicit | |
| | | Semantic | Autobiographical/ Episodic |
| Language | None | Single word | Sentence |
| Consciousness | Conscious | | Self-conscious |
| Attachment | Social smiling[i]   Stranger anxiety[ii] | Strange Situation[iii] | |

[i] Typically at around 3 months.
[ii] Typically at around 7 months.
[iii] The test is normally administered between 12 and 18 months.

social functions, for example, maternal behavior, nursing, and play (of course for later use). The ACC is the front part of the cingulate cortex located near the limbic system discussed below. Newborns are equipped with primary emotion, i.e., positive vs. negative emotions. This is due to the development of parts of the limbic system and related areas. The limbic system is the inner part of the brain, important for biological and emotional aspects, for example, the amygdala for fear/anxiety and other aspects of emotion. During the first year, part of the vagus nerve (called the "smart" vagus) develops and contributes high/low "tones" and some gut feelings relevant to attachment security/insecurity.[59] The vagus nerve system is the direct connection between the brain and various visceral organs, separate from the spinal cord. The "smart" part of the vagus nerve system, connecting the facial, mouth, and throat muscles (important for communication), modulates sympathetic arousal, including strong fight/flight reactions. The only available type of

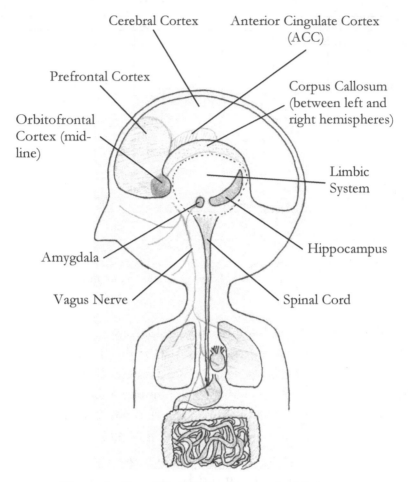

**Figure 1:  Simplified Neuroanatomical Structure**

memory during the first year is implicit, including procedural
(e.g., how to crawl) and emotional (e.g., joy with a parent, fear of
certain things).  This type of memory can be retained through life.
However, since it cannot be explicitly recalled, it would be
difficult for one to even realize that she has such memory.

During the first year, infants begin to develop attachment
patterns with primary caregivers through implicit memory.  Then,

they start to distinguish between strangers and those with whom they have an attachment relationship, leading to stranger anxiety. Note that stranger anxiety gradually disappears as infants develop cognitive skills.

If the caregiver of an infant responds to the infant in a comforting and flexible way, the infant's negative emotion (frustration) would be replaced with positive emotion (satisfaction). Over time, the infant implicitly remembers such co-regulated interactions and comes to expect the same in the future. This leads to secure attachment. An important point is that a secure infant does experience and express negative feelings; but she develops the ability to regulate them with her parent.[60]

If the caregiver ignores, rejects, and/or is controlling of the infant, the infant's negative emotion would not go away. Since overall experience becomes emotionally negative, she minimizes emotions and attachment behaviors. Over time, the infant implicitly remembers this type of interaction, which leads to avoidant attachment. During the separation episodes of Strange Situation, avoidant children do not cry. However, they show an increased heart rate and increased cortisol levels (more than secure children).[61] This demonstrates that avoidant attachment is a coping behavior.

If the caregiver's response is inconsistent and/or unpredictable, the infant will never be able to learn whether her negative emotions can be replaced with positive ones. Then, the infant would maximize emotions and attachment behaviors. She may become addicted to relationships. This is consistent with the general idea that one cannot learn from *random* reinforcement. That is, one cannot really learn anything if she is taught with correct and incorrect answers given randomly during a learning process.[62] This contrasts with both secure and avoidant children, who are successful in learning a pattern (albeit in a quite different manner). Such an infant becomes ambivalently attached. Children with ambivalent attachment may try to establish close relationships, possibly continuously throughout their lives. Unfortunately, such an excessive desire to connect may turn off other people, resulting in difficulty establishing close relationships. The three attachment patterns discussed so far are still considered "organized" because infants' responses are adaptive to the environment and not contradictory.

If the caregiver is threatening or abusive, the child develops fear as well as attachment to her. The infant is confused because she is both attracted to and running away from the caregiver. This leads to disorganized attachment. Being unable to activate both approach and withdrawal behaviors (which are contradictory), disorganized infants tend to exhibit special coping behaviors, such as freezing (see Table 1, p. 45). Disa's imaginary approach to her parents' house through the back door (p. 5) can be considered as an example of approach/withdrawal conflict. In the case of disorganized attachment, it is also possible that excessive threatening and/or abuse may become an obstacle to healthy development, including psychosocial and motor control areas. In general, their internal state can be characterized as chaotic and out of control.

Under unfortunate circumstances, such as hospitalization of their mothers, infants (especially after six months of age) may be separated from their parents for one or more weeks. It has been observed that every one of those infants goes through the same phases of separation distress: protest, despair, and detachment.[63] The same process can be observed among mourning adults as well as monkeys.[64] Thus, this seems a very strong underlying behavioral pattern shared by primates. After such an ordeal, infants would most likely be classified as disorganized.

Emotional development during the first year of life is considered to be more right-hemisphere dominant, relying on emotional, non-verbal communication and holistic meaning. When the caregiver attunes to the infant during this period, the caregiver is also supposed to primarily use her right hemisphere. Thus, the basis of attachment, and also for close relationships, is more of the right-right hemispheric communication.[65]

In any case, by the end of the first year, infants learn and implicitly remember the relationships with their caregivers, mainly through emotional interaction. This way, infants develop attachment patterns, which can be identified by the Strange Situation. Thereafter, the attachment pattern will affect one's life. Once we associate attachment patterns and implicit memory, it would be natural to consider attachment as basically environmental, not genetic or temperamental, as noted in an earlier section (Critical Discussion of Attachment Theory). However, it should not be taken that the attachment patterns are fixed. The attachment patterns at the end of the first year tend to stay, probably because the parents tend to continue their pattern of response after the first year.

### Second Year: Cognitive Development

During the second year, the hippocampus and the prefrontal cortex develop. The hippocampus is located in the limbic system. The prefrontal cortex, including the orbitofrontal cortex, is the frontal part of the cerebral cortex (or the neocortex, the outer layer of the brain). The former is essential for explicit memory and the latter for higher thinking, for example, reasoning. With the development of semantic memory, a type of explicit memory, children can now remember and recall facts and events. They also start using linguistic communication as a means to deal with various events.[66] Furthermore, they develop categorical/basic emotion, i.e., more fine-grained types of emotions, such as fear, anger, sadness, surprise, and joy.[67] These will eventually include shame and guilt at a later stage.

Although the second year marks the real beginning of cognition, it is still primitive. This is because emotion, mainly on the right hemisphere, and cognition, mainly on the left hemisphere, are not integrated.[68] Thus, even securely attached children, who develop emotion and cognition in the most balanced manner (as discussed later), would not be able to take advantage of such integration. The situation with avoidantly attached children is striking. Due to the decreased state of emotion, these children tend to rely on cognition. Some children appear to be extremely mature for their age due to the advanced state of cognition. This is consistent with a developmental analysis; people who consider the environment as not friendly would mature faster.[69] As a consequence, people with avoidant attachment tend to be highly analytical.

The development of the hippocampus is crucial for various cognitive tasks. However, if a child is under excessive stress, for example, due to threatening and/or abuse, stress hormones could destroy neurons in the hippocampus.[70] Thus, children with disorganized attachment are at risk for mental problems, including memory loss.

### Third Year and Beyond: Integration

During the third year, the corpus callosum finally develops and connects the right and left hemispheres; before this happens, children can even be seen as split-brain patients.[71] Once the corpus callosum has developed, emotion (right hemisphere) and cognition (left hemisphere) are integrated. This process is also highly relevant to associating "forms" (left hemisphere) and "contents" or "meaning" (right hemisphere). Thus, only after such cross-hemispheric connection can one really make sense. For example, children are not just understanding words associated with events (during the second year), but they start more fully making sense with emotions.

In conjunction with the development of the orbitofrontal cortex (the main area for response flexibility), hemispheric integration also enables the development of autobiographical/episodic memory, which is another type of explicit memory also integrating the sense of self or "I," for example, visualizing oneself doing a certain procedure. Such realization of self in a certain context would involve both the form (in this case, event) and meaning (in this case, emotions of self). It is not coincidence that self-consciousness develops by this stage (beginning typically at 18 months), characterized (at least partly) by the "mirror test," i.e., whether an individual is able to recognize a mark on her forehead through a mirror, say, after a nap. Due to the critical role of the first three years, these years have been referred to as the sensitive period for attachment.[72] Note that *sensitive* period is not as strong as *critical* period and thus the plasticity of the brain has not been rejected.

The integration of the left and the right hemispheres can also be discussed in the following manner. The right hemisphere, which is more dominant during the first year, is to deal with unpleasant feelings and is associated with withdrawal, invoking the sympathetic nerves.[73] This appears essential for attachment behaviors. That is, a distressed infant in general shows attachment behaviors. On the other hand, the left hemisphere, which becomes more active during the second year, is to deal with pleasant feelings and is associated with approach behaviors, invoking the parasympathetic nerves. This seems more related to exploration behaviors. Only after the integration of both hemispheres, can one balance opposite properties, including attachment and exploration. The right-left integration is also essential for reflectiveness and the ability to understand other people's minds (called the "theory of mind").[74]

Autobiographical memory and the right-left integration are the basis for people to understand and create narratives/stories (called autonoetic ability).[75] That is, to create coherent narrative, it requires the integration of the left hemisphere for organizing a narrative and the right hemisphere as the main area for autobiographical memory.[76] With this ability, one can integrate all sorts of information in a single narrative that is the basis for her own story. In fact, autonoetic ability and the ability to make sense may be the same thing.[77] While secure people can do this well, insecure people tend to have a problem with this.[78]

The emotion-cognition integration process is a crucial step for human development. Due to their balanced development of emotions, children with secure attachment would be able to fully take advantage of the process. It is in the third year that these children start making sense of many things. Note that sense-making is a complex process, and having secure attachment does not guarantee a happy life. There could be a person who is securely attached to her parents and/or children with a miserable life. There must be other factors which contribute to such a state.

However, this process would not go so smoothly for those with insecure attachment. By minimizing emotions (deactivating the right hemisphere), children with avoidant attachment tend to focus more on forms than meaning, as can be observed in the conversation between Ava and Ida. Since emotional components are essential for making sense of one's life, avoidant people tend to have more problems making sense. Their weakness in dealing with meaning would affect their close relationships in various ways. As a result, they tend to focus on the non-relationship aspects of their lives.[79] In addition, they tend to feel rejected if they have conflicts with others in terms of forms. Secure people would be able to tolerate superficial differences more comfortably. Depending on the left hemisphere, avoidant people can still be well-regulated. However, they can do so as much as they learned on their own, not dyadically with their parents. In most cases, their ability to self-regulate is more limited than it is with secure people. Due to insufficient right-left hemispheric communication, avoidant people's ability to understand and create narratives would be affected. This shows up especially when they tell stories about their childhood, such as in AAI and the family-related discussions in the story. For example, their description of childhood tends to be excessively brief, not providing sufficient information. They often fail to support their superficially positive statements. Their ability to create collaborative discourse is affected.

There is one property common to people with avoidant attachment. In general, one cannot remember her childhood before the age of two to three years old (called "infantile amnesia"). However, people with avoidant attachment in general fare much worse than others. There are at least two possibilities for this, but both of them are due to emotional underdevelopment. One is that avoidant people do not have as much emotional experience as is needed to remember their childhood well (a healthy amount of emotion is required for memory). Another possibility is due to weak narrative creation ability, i.e., due to weak right-left hemispheric integration. Considering the many striking characteristics of avoidant attachment, we chose Ava as the main character of the story. In fact, understanding avoidant attachment seems to be the key to attachment theory and the key to understanding real-life relationship issues.

Children with ambivalent attachment have a different problem. By maximizing emotions, they tend to overactivate the emotional (right) side of the hemispheric connections. This is a regulation issue. One possibility behind this situation is that ambivalent people do not register memory in the right context. That is, they may have present/past confusion and excessive recall out of context.[80] This suggests that they too have problems with autobiographical memory and thus weak self-reflection. This problem with regulation would repeat when they become parents, as the new contexts can complicate the situation even further. As a result, ambivalent people too have problems with narratives and collaborative discourse but in a way quite opposite of those with avoidant attachment. For example, when Amba recalls her childhood, she is filled with emotions and immerses herself in the situation, occasionally using the present tense. In a sense, the *virtual* relationships (e.g., memory of the relationship with a parent) dominate their minds.

Children with disorganized attachment may shut down their prefrontal cortex more frequently than others, which can lead to parental confusion, internal conflict, intrusive emotional memory, rapid shifts in state of mind, trance states, and affect regulation problems.[81] Analogous states can be observed in rats when they suffer from maternal deprivation.[82] Such a state is quite different from other insecure attachment patterns, because both avoidant and ambivalent attachment patterns are considered to be a problem with right-left hemispheric integration. However, note that a disorganized pattern is usually identified along with another pattern (i.e., secure, avoidant, or ambivalent) and thus disorganized people may share problems normally associated with other attachment patterns.

The problem with right-left hemispheric integration may even surface as a facial expression. In the story, Disa shows an asymmetrical expression. Since the left and the right halves of the face are controlled by the right and the left hemispheres, respectively, it is indeed possible to exhibit some asymmetry. In Disa's case, the fearful expression on the left half of her face may be associated with the withdrawal mind and the nostalgic expression on the right half may be associated with the approach mind.

Due to the problems discussed earlier, attachment insecurity is a risk factor for psychopathology.[83] Furthermore, the risk factors for the three insecure attachment patterns are not identical. While disorganized people in general have a higher risk, ambivalent people tend to develop depression more than avoidant people.

In addition to the description of attachment patterns discussed above, there are ways to analyze them in terms of two distinct dimensions. Here are two such attempts. In Table 6 (p. 72), attachment patterns are seen in terms of flexibility and continuity of self states.[84] The state of being flexible at one point in time seems to reflect the ability to share feelings with other people, through the right-to-right hemispheric communication. Without this ability, one would be too rigid. The state of being continuous across time (a sort of learning) appears to be associated with the ability to ground emotional experience in appropriate contexts. Without this ability, one could not learn from experience. In Table 7 (p. 72), attachment patterns are seen in terms of positive and negative views of the self and others.[85] The state of being able to view others positively must be due to the ability to share feelings, and the state of being able to view oneself positively must be associated with the ability to set oneself in context. This suggests secure people's ability to

### Table 6: Attachment Patterns
### in Terms of Flexibility and Continuity of Self State

|  |  | Flexible (at one time) | |
| --- | --- | --- | --- |
|  |  | Yes | No |
| Continuous | Yes | Secure | Avoidant |
| (across time) | No | Ambivalent | Disorganized |

### Table 7: Attachment Patterns
### in Terms of Positive/Negative View of Self/Others

|  |  | Others | |
| --- | --- | --- | --- |
|  |  | Positive | Negative |
| Self | Positive | Secure | Avoidant |
|  | Negative | Ambivalent | Disorganized |

maintain the "approach" mindset toward even negative things/events.[86] The existence of these different characterizations of attachment patterns enriches how we interpret the complexity of child-parent attachment.

By understanding the mechanism underlying attachment theory, we can gain a great deal. For example, for anyone, but especially toddlers and adolescents, self-regulation is a challenging task. When toddlers learn how to self-regulate, secure attachment is an extremely useful tool. If a toddler is securely attached to her parent, the parent can guide the toddler by comforting her as needed. Without secure attachment, toddlers must learn how to self-regulate on their own. Since self-regulation is a very difficult task, many insecure toddlers end up with an incomplete ability to do it, being easily upset.

Earlier, we mentioned that people with ambivalent attachment may be addicted to relationships. In fact, not just ambivalence, but attachment insecurity in general, may be associated with addiction of various types. For example, people with avoidant attachment may be addicted to certain materials or activities, such as research, instead of relationships.[87]  In any case, people with insecure attachment may be using various types of addiction as a substitute for love.[88]

## Parenting

Obviously, the relevance of attachment theory to parenting is enormous.  However, it is surprising that very few parents are even aware of attachment theory, although many are aware of attachment parenting and tend to assume that these are the same thing (which is not the case).  This is partly because only a handful of parenting books discuss attachment theory to a reasonable extent.[89]  In this section, we discuss additional points about the implications of attachment theory to parenting.

Secure children would explore their environment, still relying on their attachment figure.  However, one of their strengths comes from their ability to use their internalized, virtual attachment figures, if necessary.  This is the key to understanding the following.  Secure children may appear dependent because they feel comfortable using attachment figures when they are in distress.  They have the ability to ask for help if needed.[90]  On the other hand, they are actually capable of independent exploration when they are not in distress.  Since what is considered a source of distress is a learned concept, secure children can be more independent under normal circumstances. Thus, it is expected that secure children would gradually increase the range of exploration as they become comfortable.

Mothers with dismissing/avoidant attachment may show a distinct response when their children are in positive or negative contexts.  While they tend to misattune with their children's negative feelings, they may well attune much better when their children are achieving.[91]  When their children are in distress, dismissing parents may even withdraw from rather than respond to them.[92] In general, dismissing/avoidant people have a smaller window of tolerance. Once the situation turns out to be outside the window, dismissing/avoidant people may face much greater difficulty regulating themselves, compared to secure people. On the other hand, mothers with preoccupied/ambivalent attachment in general misattune with their children. However, they may attune well when their children are in fear. This would introduce relatedness through fear.[93]

Mothers with both dismissing/avoidant and preoccupied/ambivalent attachment are often characterized in terms of intrusiveness, but for different reasons.[94] Dismissing mothers may try to control their children by intruding on their personal feelings; preoccupied mothers may overstimulate their children at inappropriate times.[95]

Unlike dismissing parents, both secure and preoccupied parents are considered to be more "caring." However, it has been pointed out that the *motivation* for caring is different between these two groups. While secure parents are more altruistic, preoccupied parents are more egoistic. Preoccupied parents tend to care for children in order to satisfy their desire for a close relationship. When this caring becomes excessive, their children may not feel comfortable and become resistant, which can irritate preoccupied parents.

In the story, although Ida (one of Ava's daughters) says that her childhood experience was good, she also admits that she has rather negative views of Ava. This type of behavior can be considered as a manifestation of defensiveness associated with avoidant attachment. People like Ida may try to do just the opposite of their childhood experience.[96] For example, one might be inclined to travel for the sake of her child saying that she did not travel a lot when she was a child. This type of "syntactic" reversal (i.e., just reversing the "forms" of experience) in general would not help them resolve their real issues. The development of secure attachment is mainly based on responsive emotional communication, much of which is unconscious. Unless one realizes such an unconscious aspect and changes her underlying feelings, she tends to develop the same attachment pattern as she has with her parent, *regardless* of what she does. Karen has a relevant point: "For to be fully open to the baby's emotional needs is to become reacquainted with oneself as a baby, to re-experience the pain of being totally dependent and desperately in love and yet being shut out and feeling unwanted."[97] When it comes to parenting, it is in most cases *how* and not *what* that counts. Note that this type of syntactic reversal is not limited to avoidant parents. For example, even though Amba tries not to repeat what her mother did to her, she still ends up with a clingy child. Unconsciously, Amba must be repeating her mother's attachment patterns at the emotional level.

The distinction between secure and insecure attachments is associated with various interesting characteristics. For example, secure people are considered to be more empathic than insecure people, as can be seen in the behavior of Seca. None of the other hippos in the story is very empathic. Although a detailed discussion of empathy is beyond the scope of this book, it would be useful to include one observation on this point.[98] People with avoidant/dismissing attachment may actually develop "reverse" empathy more than the usual empathy. That is, they might expect another person to be in their own position. For example, Ava might give to her children kinds of gifts which would satisfy herself and expect them to understand her "kindness." If the children turn out to be disappointed with the gifts (which is generally the case), she would say, "You don't understand me." Ava uses this phrase in the story, though in a different situation. This may occur even between a parent and her infant child at the emotional level. For example, a parent may become upset if she *thinks* that the child does not respect her. It may well be that the child is frustrated with some physical condition which has nothing to do with the parent. A secure parent would not react that way; she would simply respond to the child and find out what is wrong without blaming the child. In the end, the important thing is not how parents perceive their children think of them but how the children really think of their parents.

In a sense, dealing with negative emotions (of oneself and one's children) may be the key to developing a secure attachment. As noted earlier, even dismissing/avoidant parents can attune with their children when they are achieving well. However, when one feels low or one's children are in distress, it may not be as easy to deal with the situation. And, this may happen at any time. If a parent can get satisfaction from responding to her child's attachment behaviors (i.e., when the child is in distress), the child is not likely to be insecure. Although it would be hard work to comfort a child in distress, the child will surely remember it with her whole body and feels warmly toward the caregiver.

Attachment is also related to issues with discipline. Some parents would promote very strict "discipline" during the first years, saying that infants are mindless and do not remember much. The authors' impression is that these parents do not understand the importance of secure attachment. We believe that it is important to focus on attachment during the first few years and then gradually emphasize discipline through dyadic regulation based on attachment. The reason that attachment insecurity is a risk factor for psychopathology must be that self-regulation is a difficult task and cannot be achieved well without the help of the trusted caregiver. For example, let us consider the case of training children not to snatch objects from other children. Some parents may enforce the "form" of not snatching by strict discipline (possibly using some reward/punishment approach).[99] This may work, at least superficially. Some other parents may remove their children from the situation (obviously they must be observing their children closely) and wait until the children understand the "meaning" of the behavior and guide them not to do so by way of empathy. But why would a child snatch an object from another child? There might be some connection between such a seemingly minor offense and other anti-social behaviors. We will come back to this point in a later section (Attachment and Meaningful Life, p. 84).

Since parenting involves so many factors, it is impossible to explain everything in terms of attachment theory. First, we can consider gender differences. For example, while avoidant boys tend to be overconfident, avoidant girls tend to be much less confident.[100] On another count, insecure children with higher academic achievement and/or higher economic power may be able to mask their attachment issues to some extent. On another front, the attachment pattern of a child is said to be influenced not only by her caregivers but also by broader contexts. For example, a good marriage is supposed to lead to more secure attachment.[101]

Another area where the importance of attachment can be confirmed is adoptions after the sensitive period (first few years). Especially when maternal deprivation and/or disorganized caregiving are involved prior to adoption, the adopting family is likely to experience hardship.[102] Psychological interventions based on behaviorism and its modern re-incarnation do not seem to work. More effective approaches seem to be based on attachment theory.[103] Such approaches would squarely face the issues involved in the attachment of the adoptee and address how to overcome the difficulty at the emotional level. The process would be lengthy and extremely difficult.

Attachment theory is often confused with "attachment parenting" and "bonding." All of these are rather different. To the authors' knowledge, no books on attachment parenting discuss important ideas in attachment theory, including attachment patterns. We will briefly compare the differences among the concepts in the following subsections.[104]

### *Attachment Parenting*

Attachment parenting is a parenting approach proposed by pediatric experts William and Martha Sears.[105] Although attachment parenting advocates might state that attachment parenting is based on the principles of attachment theory, the Sears write in their book that attachment parenting is "based on thirty-plus years of parenting our own eight children and observing moms and dads whose parenting choices seemed to make sense and whose children we liked." The book includes references to limited research results, including Ainsworth's work. However, it makes no reference to attachment theory, attachment pattern, or Bowlby.

According to the book, attachment parenting is "learning to read the cues of your baby and responding appropriately to those cues." This is indeed how a secure parent would treat her children. Furthermore, another description, "opening your mind and heart to the individual needs of your baby and letting your knowledge of your child be your guide to making on-the-spot decisions about what works best for both of you," seems consistent with the attitude of a secure parent.

However, most chapters of the book are an elaboration of the following seven attachment tools, called the Baby B's.

1.  Birth bonding

2.  Breastfeeding
3.  Babywearing
4.  Bed sharing
5.  Belief in baby's cries
6.  Balance and boundaries
7.  Beware of baby trainers

Thus, despite the authors' appeal to principled ideas consistent with secure attachment, the reader would be immersed more in the tools.  Although we are not at all against these tools (in fact, we as parents practice most of them), it must be emphasized that just doing these things (forms) may not lead to secure attachment (meaning).   A good example of such a case is found in Ainsworth's observation of a Ugandan woman, who wears, breastfeeds, and co-sleeps with her baby.[106]   Yet, the mother appears to have avoidant attachment with the baby.  We too have observed and heard of parents who "wear" a baby yet are quite controlling.  Their babies appeared to be avoidantly attached.

In general, the proponents of attachment parenting do not discuss how to *assess* the impacts of their practice.  This is quite in contrast with the research of attachment theory.  In attachment theory, assessment, such as attachment patterns, is an integral part of the research.

Some conservative parenting advisers are critical of attachment parenting, referring to the excessive leniency of the approach.  Regarding this point, it is useful to distinguish between "being in control" (e.g., by providing structure) and "controlling" (e.g., micromanagement).[107]  In general, the former is considered good and the latter, bad.  The practice of attachment parenting could be done positively or negatively in terms of both being in control and controlling.  However, the part of attachment parenting consistent with secure attachment is possible only without controlling.

In a sense, we can consider attachment parenting more as a corollary or consequence of attachment theory than as a principle on its own.  If one focuses on attachment, she would naturally adopt a parenting style not radically different from that of attachment parenting.  The parent needs to focus not on procedures but on the meaning of natural co-regulation.

## Bonding

Bonding is another term that is often confused with attachment. One particular misconception is that secure attachment requires physical bonding between the newborn baby and the mother *immediately* after delivery for a *specific* duration.[108]  This kind of misconception must have derived from a misreading of Bowlby's discussion of ethology, including sheep's biological bonding based on pheromones.  By now, it must be clear that even with this type of bonding, insecure attachment can form if parents do not respond to the baby in an appropriate manner.

## Child Care

We were very curious about the impact of center-based child care on attachment.  The existing research in general does not show that child care leads to insecure attachment.[109]  However, there is an argument that attachment research is dominated by female researchers who depend on child care.[110]  As a result, it is not desirable for those researchers to produce research pointing out problems with child care.  Thus, the literature may not provide us with unbiased information.

Now, child and human development is much more than just attachment.  As we briefly mention in our Postscript (p. 103), we as parents need to consider many other aspects as well.  It is possible that child care's impacts can be seen in areas other than attachment.[111] Two potential problems of child care as we see them are affect regulation and moral development.[112] We believe that these aspects of development call for close monitoring and guidance by a responsible person. Such an action may be necessary *at any moment*. In many child care settings, especially center-based care, it would be extremely difficult for a caregiver to be able to provide appropriate guidance exactly when needed for each of the children for whom she cares. A recent study shows that extended hours in child care can increase aggression.[113] If aggressive behaviors are not closely monitored, and thus the child is not given opportunities to regulate herself, she may not be able to develop emotional regulation successfully. Analogous points can be made for moral development. We hope that these points can be understood and addressed by parents and other caregivers.

For many parents, especially mothers, how to balance child care and work is an eternal issue. As mentioned earlier, this issue has also been affecting the course of child development research. Some researchers convince themselves that child care is a natural option, referring to the existence of group care in hunter-gatherer societies.[114] While the Efé is used as such an example, we have already discussed that the Efé parenting style is not at all like center-based child care (p. 58). Even if we can find examples of group care among hunter-gatherers, there must be a fundamental difference with center-based child care. Caregivers in center-based child care would not have as much a stake in their children as the caregivers in hunter-gatherer societies. When caregiving is done on a commercial basis, it would be extremely difficult to expect every aspect of familial care.

In his book on the negative effects of competition, Alfie Kohn credits women for counterbalancing the male dominant

competitive world.[115]    At the same time, he also regrets that
certain aspects of feminism are associated with increasing
competitiveness (both among women and with men) and a
potential decrease in caring.    Topics such as child care are
difficult to discuss openly.    However, a good hold of the topic
could lead to a better future through good relationships across
generations.


## Other Close Relationships

Attachment theory points out that the child-parent attachment
becomes the basis for all sorts of close relationships, including
those among siblings, close friends, and romantic partners.    The
current research, in general, supports this hypothesis.    Unlike
child-parent attachment, though, basically all later close
relationships are more symmetrical in terms of interaction.
Therefore, the situation is different, and possibly more complex.
However, the implications for forming a family are undeniable.
After all, a good relationship between parents is, as mentioned
earlier, a desirable environment for child-parent attachment.

    In general, people with secure attachment have longer-lasting
close relationships with others.[116]    It has been reported that a
male and a female rarely form a romantic relationship if they both
have avoidant attachment.[117]    On the other hand, a male and a
female can become stable over time if they are avoidant and
ambivalent, respectively, even though such a couple would
continue to argue.[118]    In fact, it appears that people with avoidant
attachment do not generally develop deep relationships.    For
example, the interaction between Ava and Ida appears to show
some avoidant-avoidant conflict.    When two people with
avoidant attachment agree on certain things, they can get along
well; on the other hand, if they disagree, they would feel

immediately uncomfortable and rejected.  Since people with avoidant attachment loathe rejection, they would unconsciously avoid such occasions.   Furthermore, analogous to the corresponding child-parent relationship (p. 74), when the partner is in distress, an avoidant person may withdraw from the situation instead of responding to the partner.  However, the interaction between Ava and Dana appears somewhat different.  This is because Ava was able to focus more on the meaning instead of the form.

Some further applications of attachment theory outside the usual close relationships include the following.  First, the relationship to self is used to explain the connection between secure attachment and mindfulness (see Attachment and Meaningful Life, p. 84).  Second, modern families are said to be anxiously attached to society.[119]  Or, certain societies may well be promoting insecurity of various sorts directly or indirectly.  Although these are not considered attachment theory proper, when the interaction involved in attachment is seen in terms of complex systems ideas, it seems to make some sense.[120]

The relevance of attachment theory is limited to *close* relationships.  As such, it does not apply to relationships between strangers.  For this reason, it is in general impossible to recognize attachment patterns by observing interaction among strangers, for example, during conversation at a party.  However, it may well be possible to identify the same person's attachment pattern if she is seen interacting with her family members.

# Bereavement

The discussion so far can be applied to understanding how people cope with bereavement.  One might think that strong attachment is problematic when the attachment figure is no longer available, for example, due to death. However, it turns out to be that people with secure attachment are more resilient when this happens.[121]

Securely attached people internalize and carry their virtual attachment figures with them for the rest of their lives. This way, even when these attachment figures are no longer *physically* available, they can behave as if they were available *virtually*. Thus, secure people may be better able to deal with solitude.[122] This point is an interesting connection to the teaching of Buddhism, i.e., "detachment." That is, secure attachment can be considered as a basis for future detachment (in a positive sense), although the real meaning of detachment in Buddhism must be deeper. Let us also recall that real independence can develop through secure attachment, which might appear as a sign of dependence to some naive eyes. On the other hand, forcing independence too early could lead to later dependence. These superficially contradicting phenomena may be understood as an instance of the Taoism teaching, which tends to sound paradoxical, for example, "action without action."

Resilience to hardship can also be extended to the situation facing one's own death. Note that one's life may be terminated for a variety of reasons *at any moment*. For most of us, death is a difficult process and is a cause of great distress. Then, the process would naturally invoke attachment behaviors.[123] Thus, whether or not one is securely attached would make a big difference.

## Attachment and Meaningful Life

In this section, we integrate the discussion in earlier sections and make the connection between attachment and meaningful life, mainly based on Daniel Siegel's work.[124] The main idea is summarized as a conceptual framework in Figure 2 (p. 86). One's ability to make sense of her life depends on attachment directly and indirectly. The direct path involves the role of secure attachment as the source of generally satisfying close relationships and resilience to hardships. The indirect path involves the ability to reflect cognitively *and* emotionally, which is a property of secure attachment, as the source of accurate, objective, and often positive meaning-creation processes. This idea will be explored below in more detail.

By the end of the first year, an infant would develop the basic pattern of attachment. We discussed in earlier sections that secure attachment is due to healthy emotional development (especially around the limbic system). This is a result of healthy infant-caregiver co-regulation, involving the responsiveness of the caregiver. Beginning in the third year (age 2 in Table 5, p. 61), most securely attached children would begin the process of integrating cognition with emotion (especially around the orbitofrontal cortex and across the corpus callosum).[125] Through this process, they also develop the ability to reflect emotionally and cognitively. By emotional reflectiveness, we refer to the ability to feel felt. By cognitive reflectiveness, we refer to the ability to explicitly think of one's own conscious thinking. When a person creates a cohesive narrative during an AAI session, she must be employing both types of reflectiveness.

As we discussed in earlier sections, secure attachment in general leads to satisfying close relationships and resilience to hardship by invoking their internal working models of the attachment figures. These properties are essential for a meaningful life. Although this point cannot be proven, we know this from examples in real life and literature. Since this is the most obvious element behind the relationship-meaning

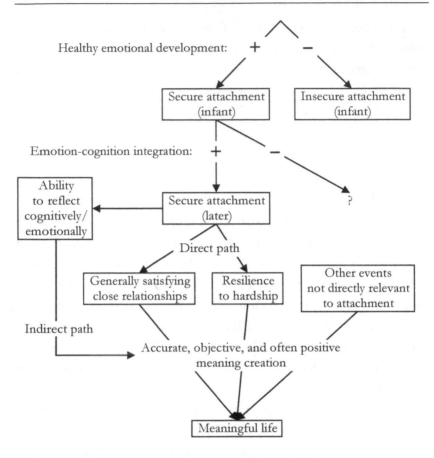

**Figure 2: Attachment and Meaningful Life**

connection, it is called the *direct path* and indicated as such in Figure 2.

For many people, satisfying close relationships and resilience to hardship may be sufficient for relating attachment and meaningful life. However, Siegel suggests a more general way of connecting the two. That is, the ability to reflect emotionally *and* cognitively would let securely attached people accurately, objectively, and often positively create meaning out of events not necessarily relevant to attachment. This depends on one's holistic assessment (i.e., value assignment) of her intentions and their interaction with the environment.[126]   Such holistic assessment then relies on emotions.   Emotions also direct her resources for achieving goals through flow of activation or energy.[127]   Thus, the meaning creation process is basically an emotional process.   Since this aspect of the relationship-meaning connection does not depend on the internal working model, and thus not as obvious as the direct path, it is called the *indirect path* and indicated as such in Figure 2.

If one is able to make sense through secure attachment, i.e., attunement with other people, she may also be able to make sense through attunement with herself.[128]   This state of attunement with oneself has been proposed as one of the main properties of mindfulness meditation.[129]   Since mindfulness is associated with self-understanding and self-integration, the three concepts of making sense, secure attachment, and mindfulness must be closely related.[130]   All of these promote good relationships, resilience, and well-being.[131]   It would be an interesting practice if one can compensate for her insecure attachment through mindfulness meditation.

On the other hand, as the greatest source of insecurity, severe maternal deprivation (especially after 6 months of age) is by all means an ordeal for an infant.  As Bowlby has pointed out, such an infant has a higher risk of turning out to be a delinquent or criminal with no sense of (negative) meaning for their antisocial acts, such as stealing, violence, sexual misbehavior, etc.  Such a person may be symbolizing the lack of maternal love purely *syntactically* in various distorted *forms*.  That is, she may employ antisocial behaviors to attract the attention of others.  Due to the lack of co-regulation with her caregivers, the person would have a problem with self-regulation as well, which can aggravate the situation.  Even without the history of maternal deprivation, it may be possible to trace instances of minor offenses, such as snatching, to some sort of attachment insecurity and the lack of appropriate meaning associated with the action. A securely attached person would be able to associate appropriate meanings to antisocial activities.

Here is another point. Since people with insecure attachment tend to have problems with emotions, they often depend on external value systems. They might be more inclined to work hard to be recognized based on what other people have established. They tend to depend on extrinsic, rather than intrinsic, motivation. As a result, their meaning creation process can be more vulnerable.

Although we have been discussing that secure people can in general make more sense out of life, this point needs to be qualified. For example, one might ask the following questions. Are there securely attached people who are not making sense of their lives? Are insecurely attached people not making sense at all? Although securely attached people are in a better position to make sense of their lives due to their ability to reflect, this is by no means a guarantee. There are so many factors involved here. There may well be cases where even securely attached people cannot make sense. For example, what if Seca in the story develops a brain tumor which affects her emotional communication? Such a problem could turn upside down the life of even a securely attached person.

In terms of making sense, those with insecure attachment generally fare much worse. But it does not mean that they cannot make sense. For example, it might be possible that some individual may derive meaning exclusively from her superior accomplishments. However, it would be difficult for most people to be able to maintain superiority without a hint of failure. Insecurely attached people may well suffer greatly from a seemingly minor obstacle. Furthermore, despite continuous achievements, insecurely attached people may still suffer from poor close relationships.

Thus, the difference between being securely and insecurely attached appears to be huge. Nevertheless, this point often goes unnoticed. This is because the origin of the difference is in implicit memory, which cannot be consciously recalled. In order to make up, insecurely attached people must be able to recognize and accept their attachment pattern and reflect on it in their lives. In the story, Ava started this process toward the end of her life. We believe that such a step is essential for Ava to be able to make at least some sense of her life. Without such a move, insecurely attached people have a higher risk of various psychological and even physical problems, which could be described as "of unknown origin." For example, Charles Darwin's suffering from a strange series of symptoms has been traced by Bowlby to his attachment issues.[132]

Before closing this section, let us consider the story, "The Little Match Girl" by Hans Christian Andersen.[133] In the story, a match girl fails to sell matches and cannot go home, because her father would beat her if she returns with no money. On a street, she tries to warm herself by lighting matches. Magically, she sees illusions, including her grandmother, who loved her unconditionally when alive. The next morning, people find the girl frozen to death. But she had a smile as she was finally able to join her grandmother. While it is indeed a sad story, it is also possible to consider that the little match girl was able to make sense due to her attachment to her grandmother. Although the girl did not have much of a chance to develop satisfying close relationships later in her life, she definitely was coping with incredible hardship by thinking of her grandmother. Even before dying, she was able to try to get the best out of those matches. If she had not had the attachment to her grandmother, the story would have been very different. So, although it is sad, we still see some sort of hope in the story. That seems to be what makes this story great.

## Conclusion

In this commentary, we point out that secure child-parent attachment is essential for making sense of one's life. To do so, we explore attachment theory and related topics in some detail. Although our journey is inevitably informal and incomplete, we hope that the discussion provides interesting material for further understanding of the issue. Attachment theory offers deep insight into how child-caregiver relationships form and how such relationships could affect later close relationships, including those with subsequent children. To develop secure attachment, parents/caregivers must be able to respond to their children's feelings, often expressed nonverbally, and to co-regulate with them. Simply following certain "forms" of parental practice may not result in secure attachment. It is amazing how the beginning of life, which cannot even be remembered, can make a difference later in our lives.

Attachment theory is one of the most powerful ideas for understanding close relationships. By realizing one's attachment pattern, one will be able to realize the unconscious, emotional aspects of behavior underlying close relationships. As in the case of Ava in the story, one may be able to understand why things are a certain way around her and may be able to make some sense even toward the end of her life. Hopefully, one would realize attachment-related issues earlier in life so that one can adjust accordingly. Even securely attached people can benefit from attachment theory by accommodating their relatives and friends, who may be insecurely attached.

We believe that attachment theory is a perfect starting point for exploring parenting principles, because many aspects of later development (see Postscript, p. 103) depend on child-parent attachment. For example, emotional development and self-regulation would heavily depend on attachment, shifting from dyadic to self-regulation.[134] Most toddlers have a strong desire for various things which are not acceptable from their parents' point of view. When the toddlers fail to get the desired items/actions, they tend to express their disappointment in various ways. With secure attachment, a toddler and her parents would be able to co-regulate the toddler's emotional roller coaster. In a similar fashion, moral development would depend on children's ability to regulate first emotions and then cognition.[135] Finally, even ideas not directly related to emotions, for example, complex systems thinking and mindfulness, may never make sense unless children learn to view various things in a balanced way, where intuition (more right hemispheric) is valued as much as analytic ability (more left hemispheric).[136]

# Notes

## Introduction

1. In this commentary, "making sense of one's life" is understood as the same thing as living a "meaningful life." The notion of "making sense" may be interpreted more broadly as just understanding one's life (as in the Longman Advanced American Dictionary) or more narrowly as discovering the underlying cause-effect relation (e.g., Siegel, 1999). Our use lies somewhere between these two extremes. That is, while it would not be enough to understand one's life to really make sense of it, a meaningful life may well be possible without discovering the cause-effect relation underlying one's life.

2. Karen (1994). An earlier version (1990) of the book as a journal article is available on-line (as of January 2008) at: http://www.psychology.sunysb.edu/attachment/online/karen.pdf

3. Siegel (1999).

4. Cassidy and Shaver (1999).

5. Grossmann et al. (2005); Sroufe (2005); NICHD Early Child Care Research Network (2005); Carter et al. (2005); Rholes and Simpson (2004).

## Meaningful Life and Close Relationships

6. Siegel (1999); Freeman (2000).

7. Cozolino (2006); Greenspan and Benderly (1997); Stern (1985).

8. A discussion of different types of memory and their connection to emotion and attachment are summarized in Siegel (1999).

## Attachment Theory

9. For Bowlby and Ainsworth's original work, see Karen (1994).

10. Concisely summarized in Davies (2004, pp. 55-60).

11. Concisely summarized in Feeney and Collins (2004).

12. Siegel (2007, p. 213).

13. For intimacy-independence balance, see Pietromonaco et al. (2004, pp. 271-272). For negative and positive emotions, see Siegel (1999, pp. 137-138).

14. Concisely summarized in Collins et al. (2004).

15. For example, Schore (1994) and Siegel (1999).

16. For example, Karr-Morse and Wiley (1997), Hughes (2006), and Davies (2004).

17. Karen (1994). Attachment theory is contrasted with object relation theory, especially with respect to the role of fantasy.

18. Karen (1994, p. 102).
19. Karen (1994, pp. 170-173).
20. For co-regulation, see Fogel (1993). For mutual regulation, see Tronick (2007). For affect attunement, see Stern (1985).

## Attachment Patterns

21. Karen (1994, p. 225).
22. Karen (1994, p. 225).
23. George and Solomon (1999, p. 654).
24. Belsky (1999).
25. For example, the Minnesota studies lead by Alan Sroufe, summarized in Karen (1994). See also Thompson (1999).
26. Karen (1994, p. 382).
27. Siegel (1999, pp. 317-318).
28. For example, van Ijzendoorn and Sagi (1999).
29. Kibbutz cases are discussed in George and Solomon (1999, pp. 721-724). German cases are discussed in Karen (1994, pp. 261-266).

## Strange Situation

30. There are other infant attachment measurement methods. See Solomon and George (1999).
31. Karen (1994, p. 223).
32. Grossmann et al. (1999, p. 765).

## Attachment Continuity

33. See, e.g., Belsky (2005). For one of the most recent results, see Sroufe (2005).
34. Discussed, e.g., in Karen (1994, Ch. 24) and Siegel (1999, p. 78).
35. Discussed, e.g., in Karen (1994).
36. Discussed, e.g., in Siegel (1999, pp. 91-92). Although Siegel (2007, p. 204) suggests that one can "earn" secure attachment, for example, through therapy, it seems that this may not happen so easily. When an adult is assessed as secure despite her insecure (infant) attachment history, significant events are likely to have happened relatively early in her life, probably before adolescence.
37. Karen (1994, pp. 210, 231).
38. Discussed, e.g., in Karen (1994, p. 389), citing Klaus Grossmann. Such a consolidation process may never be complete. If so, even adults may carry multiple attachment patterns with them, which may be referred to in different contexts.

## Adult Attachment Interview (AAI)

39. Summarized in Hesse (1999).   Note that there are other ways of measuring adult attachment, e.g., based on self-report.   For this, see Crowell et al. (1999).
40. Taken from Hesse (1999).
41. For example, Siegel (1999).
42. Grice (1975).
43. Discussed, e.g., in Karen (1994).
44. Karen (1994, p. 219).

## Critical Discussion of Attachment Theory

45. For example, Cohen (1999), Rowe (1994), and Hamer and Copeland (1998).
46. Harris (1998).
47. Kagan (1984).
48. Bokhorst et al. (2003).
49. Discussed, e.g., in Karen (1994).
50. For example, Ridley (2003).
51. This point is in Biringen (2004).   Additional resources against Harris are summarized in Evans (2004, p. 252).
52. See Vaughn and Bost (1999) and Karen (1994, pp. 304, 308-310).
53. For Efé and Kisii descriptions, see Tronick (2007, Ch. 8 Efé, Ch. 10 Kisii).
54. For a discussion of group care, see Hrdy (1999).
55. Karen (1994, esp. Ch. 19).
56. Karen (1994, pp. 166-169, 327).

## Mechanisms Underlying Attachment

57. For example, Schore (1994), Siegel (1999), and Cozolino (2006).
58. There are opinions that there is no mental representation (Freeman, 2000).   For our purposes, it would be sufficient to assume that attachment patterns are formed and internalized in ourselves.
59. Cozolino (2006), citing S. Porges and others.
60. Karen (1994, p. 245).
61. For example, Fox and Card (1999).
62. Karen (1994, p. 377).
63. See, for example, Kobak (1999, p. 24), citing the original work of J. Robertson and J. Bowlby.
64. For mourning adults, see Fraley and Shaver (1999, p. 736).   For monkeys, see Suomi (1999, pp. 186-187).
65. Siegel (1999, p. 153).
66. For example, Nelson (1996).
67. Concisely summarized in Lewis (2000).
68. This type of right-left dichotomy is an oversimplification and in fact a controversial topic.   For example, language actually uses both

hemispheres. However, more prominent features of language, e.g., syntax, are still mainly processed in the left hemisphere and contextual and prosodic information are processed in the right hemisphere. For more details, see Siegel (1999) and Cozolino (2006).

69. Simpson (1999, p. 131) and Belsky (1999, p. 148), referring to "life history theory."
70. Siegel (1999, p. 59), citing J. Bremner and M. Narayan.
71. Siegel (1999, p. 187).
72. Siegel (1999, p. 194).
73. Siegel (1999, pp. 151-152, 279).
74. Siegel (1999, p. 188).
75. Siegel (1999, p. 331).
76. Siegel (2007, p. 143).
77. Relevant discussions in Engel (2005).
78. Main (1991/1993).
79. Karen (1994, p. 316).
80. Siegel (1999, pp. 105-106).
81. Siegel (2007, p. 204).
82. Siegel (1999, p. 84).
83. Siegel (1999, pp. 68, 84, 86), citing other sources.
84. Siegel (1999, pp. 237-238).
85. Kazui and Endo (2005, p. 151), citing K. Bartholomew.
86. Siegel (2007, pp. 222-223).
87. Karen (1994, p. 384).
88. Cozolino (2006, p. 113).

## Parenting

89. For example, Biringen (2004), Siegel and Hartzell (2003), and Lieberman (1993). Some other parenting books (e.g., Kohn, 2005; Leo, 2005) are consistent with the ideas in attachment theory. However, without awareness of their attachment types, insecurely attached people may have difficulty truly following the lessons in such books. On the other hand, by understanding the basics of attachment theory, they could recognize and compensate for the missing elements. The importance of secure attachment is also discussed in another book on the child-parent relationship (Pearce, 1977) without reference to attachment theory.
90. Karen (1994, p. 383).
91. Karen (1994, p. 357).
92. Feeney and Collins (2004, p. 316).
93. Karen (1994, p. 357).
94. Karen (1994, pp. 376-377, 416).
95. Kazui and Endo (2005, p. 197) state that dismissing/avoidant parents overstimulate during the first half of the first year, and then understimulate during the latter half, while preoccupied/ambivalent

parents understimulate during the first half of the first year, then overstimulate during the latter half.

96. A similar idea is discussed in Karen (1994, p. 379).
97. Karen (1994, p. 375).
98. Regarding empathy, see, e.g., Hoffman (2000).
99. Kohn (1993) points out the problems associated with rewards and punishments.
100. Karen (1994, p. 378).
101. Kazui and Endo (2005, p. 191).
102. For example, Hughes (2006).
103. For example, Hughes (2006).
104. For more discussion, see Mercer (2006).
105. Sears and Sears (2001). The quotes are from pages ix and 2. The Baby B's are on pages 5-7.
106. Karen (1994, p. 142).
107. Grolnick (2003).
108. Karen (1994, Note 8 on p. 451). Sears and Sears (2001, p. 36) refer to a book by M. Klaus and J. Kennell.
109. NICHD Early Child Care Research Network (1997), also included in NICHD Early Child Care Research Network (2005). But slightly high insecurity has also been noted for children in child care (Karen, 1994, Ch. 22).
110. Karen (1994); Robertson (2003).
111. Robertson (2003).
112. For affect regulation, see, e.g., Schore (1994). For moral development, see, e.g., Hoffman (2000), who points out that the cognitive aspects of moral development appear after the age of three.
113. NICHD Early Child Care Research Network (2003), also included in NICHD Early Child Care Research Network (2005).
114. Hrdy (1999).
115. Kohn (1986).

## Other Close Relationships

116. Karen (1994, p. 387).
117. Bretherton and Munholland (1999, p. 107), citing P. Shaver and C. Hazan.
118. Feeney (1999, p. 364).
119. Karen (1994, p. 413).
120. For the connection between attachment and complex systems, see Siegel (1999).

## Bereavement

121. For example, Fraley and Shaver (1999).
122. Karen (1994, pp. 383-384).

123. Karen (1994, p. 385) mentions that Elisabeth Kübler-Ross incorporated attachment ideas in her famous book, *On Death and Dying*.

## Attachment and Meaningful Life

124. Siegel (1999).
125. One question here is what would happen to securely attached *infants* who fail to integrate cognition and emotion (indicated as "?" in Fig. 2, p. 86). Although Siegel does not discuss such a case, we suspect that this indeed is a possibility. People in this class might be able to feel felt but would not be able to reflect consciously. If they go through AAI, without the emotion-cognition integration, they might be classified as insecure. However, they may well be able to develop close relationships very well due to their healthy emotional development.
126. Siegel (1999, pp. 136, 139-140, 245); Freeman (2000, pp. 8-9). See also Siegel (2007, p. 176) for the connection between intention and mirror neurons. Mirror neurons fire both when one performs certain actions intentionally and when one sees the same intentional actions (e.g., Rizzolatti and Arbib, 1998). Another relevant point about the mismatch between desire and expected outcome is in Harris (2000).
127. Siegel (1999, p. 263).
128. Siegel (1999, p. 266). More about the concept of "attunement" with oneself and mindfulness in Siegel (2007).
129. Siegel (2007). He also proposes that mirror neurons are involved in attunement and mindfulness. For the discussion of mindfulness and other types of meditation, see Goleman (1988).
130. Siegel (1999, p. 314; 2007, p. 206).
131. Siegel (2007, pp. 26, 41).
132. Karen (1994, pp. 426-427).
133. English translation available (as of January 2008) at: http://www.andersen.sdu.dk/vaerk/hersholt/TheLittleMatchGirl_e.html

## Conclusion

134. For example, Sroufe (1996).
135. For example, Hoffman (2000).
136. For example, Varela et al. (1991). Although the ideas of complex systems and mindfulness may appear rather different, these two are beautifully integrated in Varela et al.

# References

Belsky, J. 2005. The Developmental and Evolutionary Psychology of Intergenerational Transmission of Attachment. In *Attachment and bonding: a new synthesis*, eds. Carol Sue Carter et al., 167-198. Cambridge, MA: MIT Press.

Belsky, Jay. 1999. Modern Evolutionary Theory and Patterns of Attachment. In *Handbook of attachment: theory, research, and clinical applications*, eds. Jude Cassidy and Phillip R. Shaver, 141-161. New York: Guilford Press.

Biringen, Zeynep. 2004. *Raising a secure child: creating an emotional connection between you and your child.* New York: Perigee Book.

Bokhorst, Caroline L., Bakermans-Kranenburg, Marian J., Fearon, R. M. Pasco, Van IJzendoorn, Marinus H., Fonagy, Peter, and Schuengel, Carlo. 2003. The Importance of Shared Environment in Mother–Infant Attachment Security: A Behavioral Genetic Study. *Child Development* 74(6):1769-1782.

Bretherton, Inge and Munholland, Kristine A. 1999. Internal Working Models in Attachment Relationships: A Construct Revised. In *Handbook of attachment: theory, research, and clinical applications*, eds. Jude Cassidy and Phillip R. Shaver, 89-111. New York: Guilford Press.

Carter, Carol Sue, Ahnert, L., Gossmann, K. E., B., Hrdy S., Lamb, M. E., Porges, S. W., and Sachser, N., eds. 2005. *Attachment and bonding: a new synthesis.* Cambridge, MA: MIT Press.

Cassidy, Jude and Shaver, Phillip R., eds. 1999. *Handbook of attachment: theory, research, and clinical applications.* New York: Guilford Press.

Cohen, David B. 1999. *Stranger in the nest: do parents really shape their child's personality, intelligence, or character?* New York: John Wiley & Sons.

Collins, Nancy L., Guichard, AnaMarie C., Ford, Maire B., and Feeney, Brooke C. 2004. Working Models of Attachment: New Developments and Emerging Themes. In *Adult attachment: theory, research, and clinical implications*, eds. W. Steven Rholes and Jeffry A. Simpson, 196-239. New York: Guilford Press.

Cozolino, Louis J. 2006. *The neuroscience of human relationships: attachment and the developing social brain.* New York: Norton.

Crowell, Judith A., Fraley, R. Chris, and Shaver, Phillip R. 1999. Measurement of Individual Differences in Adolescent and Adult Attachment. In *Handbook of attachment: theory, research, and clinical applications*, eds. Jude Cassidy and Phillip R. Shaver, 434-465. New York: Guilford Press.

Davies, Douglas. 2004. *Child development: a practitioner's guide*, 2nd ed. New York: Guilford Press.

Engel, Susan. 2005. *Real kids: creating meaning in everyday life.* Cambridge, MA: Harvard University Press.

Evans, Robert. 2004. *Family matters: how schools can cope with the crisis in childrearing.* San Francisco: Jossey-Bass.

Feeney, Brooke C. and Collins, Nancy L. 2004. Interpersonal Safe Haven and Secure Base Caregiving Processes in Adulthood. In *Adult attachment: theory, research, and clinical implications*, eds. W. Steven Rholes and Jeffry A. Simpson, 300-338. New York: Guilford Press.

Feeney, Judith A. 1999. Adult Romantic Attachment and Couple Relationships. In *Handbook of attachment: theory, research, and clinical applications*, eds. Jude Cassidy and Phillip R. Shaver, 355-377. New York: Guilford Press.

Fogel, Alan. 1993. *Developing through relationships: origins of communication, self, and culture.* Chicago: University of Chicago Press.

Fox, Nathan A. and Card, Judith A. 1999. Psychophysiological Measures in the Study of Attachment. In *Handbook of attachment: theory, research, and clinical applications*, eds. Jude Cassidy and Phillip R. Shaver, 226-245. New York: Guilford Press.

Fraley, R. Chris and Shaver, Phillip R. 1999. Loss and Bereavement: Attachment Theory and Recent Controversies Concerning "Grief Work" and the Nature of Detachment. In *Handbook of attachment: theory, research, and clinical applications*, eds. Jude Cassidy and Phillip R. Shaver, 735-759. New York: Guilford Press.

Freeman, Walter J. 2000. *How brains make up their minds.* New York: Columbia University Press.

George, Carol and Solomon, Judith. 1999. Attachment and Caregiving: The Caregiving Behavioral System. In *Handbook of attachment: theory, research, and clinical applications*, eds. Jude Cassidy and Phillip R. Shaver, 649-670. New York: Guilford Press.

Goleman, Daniel. 1988. *The meditative mind: the varieties of meditative experience.* Los Angeles: J.P. Tarcher.

Greenspan, Stanley I. and Benderly, Beryl Lieff. 1997. *The growth of the mind: and the endangered origins of intelligence.* Reading, MA: Addison-Wesley Pub.

Grice, H. P. 1975. Logic and Conversation. In *Syntax and Semantics, Vol. 3: Speech Acts*, eds. Peter Cole and Jerry Morgan, 305-315. New York: Academic Press.

Grolnick, Wendy S. 2003. *The psychology of parental control: how well-meant parenting backfires.* Mahwah, NJ: L. Erlbaum Associates.

Grossmann, Klaus E., Grossmann, Karin, and Zimmermann, Peter. 1999. A Wider View of Attachment and Exploration: Stability and Change during the Years of Immaturity. In *Handbook of attachment: theory, research, and clinical applications*, eds. Jude Cassidy and Phillip R. Shaver, 760-786. New York: Guilford Press.

Grossmann, Klaus E., Grossmann, Karin, and Waters, Everett, eds. 2005. *Attachment from infancy to adulthood: the major longitudinal studies.* New York: Guilford Press.

Hamer, Dean H. and Copeland, Peter. 1998. *Living with our genes: why they matter more than you think*. New York: Doubleday.

Harris, Judith Rich. 1998. *The nurture assumption: why children turn out the way they do*. New York: Free Press.

Harris, Paul L. 2000. Understanding Emotion. In *Handbook of emotions*, eds. Michael Lewis and Jeannette M. Haviland-Jones, 281-292. New York: Guilford Press.

Hesse, Erik. 1999. The Adult Attachment Interview: Historical and Current Perspectives. In *Handbook of attachment: theory, research, and clinical applications*, eds. Jude Cassidy and Phillip R. Shaver, 395-433. New York: Guilford Press.

Hoffman, Martin L. 2000. *Empathy and moral development: implications for caring and justice*. Cambridge: Cambridge University Press.

Hrdy, Sarah Blaffer. 1999. *Mother nature: maternal instincts and how they shape the human species*. New York: Ballantine Books.

Hughes, Daniel A. 2006. *Building the bonds of attachment: awakening love in deeply troubled children*, 2nd ed. Lanham, MD: Jason Aronson.

Kagan, Jerome. 1984. *The nature of the child*. New York: Basic Books.

Karen, Robert. 1994. *Becoming attached: unfolding the mystery of the infant-mother bond and its impact on later life*. New York: Warner Books.

Karr-Morse, Robin and Wiley, Meredith S. 1997. *Ghosts from the nursery: tracing the roots of violence*. New York: The Atlantic Monthly Press.

Kazui, Miyuki and Endo, Toshihiko, eds. 2005. *Atacchimento: Shogai-ni Wataru Kizuna (Attachment: Bonding Through Life)*. Kyoto, Japan: Mineruba Shobo.

Kobak, Roger. 1999. The Emotional Dynamics of Disruptions in Attachment Relationships: Implications for Theory, Research, and Clinical Intervention. In *Handbook of attachment: theory, research, and clinical applications*, eds. Jude Cassidy and Phillip R. Shaver, 21-43. New York: Guilford Press.

Kohn, Alfie. 1986. *No contest: the case against competition*. Boston: Houghton Mifflin.

Kohn, Alfie. 1993. *Punished by rewards: the trouble with gold stars, incentive plans, A's, praise, and other bribes*. Boston: Houghton Mifflin Co.

Kohn, Alfie. 2005. *Unconditional parenting: moving from rewards and punishments to love and reason*, 1st Atria Books hardcover ed. New York: Atria Books.

Leo, Pam. 2005. *Connection parenting: parenting through connection instead of coercion, through love instead of fear*. Deadwood, OR: Wyatt-MacKenzie Pub., Inc.

Lewis, Michael. 2000. The Emergence of Human Emotions. In *Handbook of emotions*, eds. Michael Lewis and Jeannette M. Haviland-Jones, 265-280. New York: Guilford Press.

Lieberman, Alicia F. 1993. *The emotional life of the toddler*. New York: Free Press.

Main, Mary. 1991/1993. Metacognitive knowledge, metacognitive monitoring, and singular (coherent) vs. multiple (incoherent) model of attachment: Findings and directions for future research. In *Attachment across the life cycle*, eds. Colin Murray Parkes, J. S. Hinde, and Peter Marris, 127-159. London: Routledge.

Mercer, Jean. 2006. *Understanding attachment: parenting, child care, and emotional development.* Westport, CT: Praeger Publishers.

Nelson, Katherine. 1996. *Language in cognitive development: emergence of the mediated mind.* Cambridge: Cambridge University Press.

NICHD Early Child Care Research Network. 1997. The Effects of Infant Child Care on Infant-Mother Attachment Security: Results of the NICHD Study of Early Child Care. *Child Development* 68(5):860-879.

NICHD Early Child Care Research Network. 2003. Does Amount of Time Spent in Child Care Predict Socioemotional Adjustment during the Transition to Kindergarten? *Child Development* 74(4):976-1005.

NICHD Early Child Care Research Network. 2005. *Child care and child development: results from the NICHD study of early child care and youth development.* New York: Guilford Press.

Pearce, Joseph Chilton. 1977. *Magical child: rediscovering nature's plan for our children,* 1st ed. New York: Dutton.

Pietromonaco, Paula R., Greenwood, Dara, and Barrett, Lisa Feldman. 2004. Conflict in Adult Close Relationships: An Attachment Perspective. In *Adult attachment: theory, research, and clinical implications,* eds. W. Steven Rholes and Jeffry A. Simpson, 267-299. New York: Guilford Press.

Rholes, W. Steven and Simpson, Jeffry A., eds. 2004. *Adult attachment: theory, research, and clinical implications.* New York: Guilford Press.

Ridley, Matt. 2003. *Nature via nurture: genes, experience, and what makes us human,* 1st ed. New York: HarperCollins.

Rizzolatti, Giacomo and Arbib, Michael A. 1998. Language within our grasp. *Trends in Neurosciences* 21(5):188-194.

Robertson, Brian C. 2003. *Day care deception: what the child care establishment isn't telling us.* San Francisco: Encounter Books.

Rowe, David C. 1994. *The limits of family influence: genes, experience, and behavior.* New York: Guilford Press.

Schore, Allan N. 1994. *Affect regulation and the origin of the self: the neurobiology of emotional development.* Hillsdale, NJ: Lawrence Erlbaum Associates.

Sears, William and Sears, Martha. 2001. *The attachment parenting book: a commonsense guide to understanding and nurturing your baby.* Boston: Little, Brown and Company.

Siegel, Daniel J. 1999. *The developing mind: toward a neurobiology of interpersonal experience.* New York: Guilford Press.

Siegel, Daniel J. and Hartzell, Mary. 2003. *Parenting from the inside out: how a deeper self-understanding can help you raise children who thrive.* New York: J.P. Tarcher/Putnam.

Siegel, Daniel J. 2007. *The mindful brain: reflection and attunement in the cultivation of well-being.* New York: W.W. Norton.

Simpson, Jeffry A. 1999. Attachment Theory in Modern Evolutionary Perspective. In *Handbook of attachment: theory, research, and clinical applications,* eds. Jude Cassidy and Phillip R. Shaver, 115-140. New York: Guilford Press.

Solomon, Judith and George, Carol. 1999. The Measurement of Attachment Security in Infancy and Childhood. In *Handbook of attachment: theory, research, and clinical applications*, eds. Jude Cassidy and Phillip R. Shaver, 287-316. New York: Guilford Press.

Sroufe, L. Alan. 1996. *Emotional development: the organization of emotional life in the early years*. Cambridge: Cambridge University Press.

Sroufe, L. Alan. 2005. *The development of the person: the Minnesota study of risk and adaptation from birth to adulthood*. New York: Guilford Press.

Stern, Daniel N. 1985. *The interpersonal world of the infant: a view from psychoanalysis and developmental psychology*. New York: Basic Books.

Suomi, Stephen J. 1999. Attachment in Rhesus Monkeys. In *Handbook of attachment: theory, research, and clinical applications*, eds. Jude Cassidy and Phillip R. Shaver, 181-197. New York: Guilford Press.

Thompson, Ross A. 1999. Early Attachment and Later Development. In *Handbook of attachment: theory, research, and clinical applications*, eds. Jude Cassidy and Phillip R. Shaver, 265-286. New York: Guilford Press.

Tronick, Edward. 2007. *The neurobehavioral and social emotional development of infants and children*. New York: W. W. Norton & Co.

van Ijzendoorn, Marinus H. and Sagi, Abraham. 1999. Cross-Cultural Patterns of Attachment: Universal and Contextual Dimensions. In *Handbook of attachment: theory, research, and clinical applications*, eds. Jude Cassidy and Phillip R. Shaver, 713-734. New York: Guilford Press.

Varela, Francisco J., Thompson, Evan, and Rosch, Eleanor. 1991. *The embodied mind: cognitive science and human experience*. Cambridge, MA: MIT Press.

Vaughn, Brian E. and Bost, Kelly K. 1999. Attachment and Temperament: Redundant, Independent, or Interacting Influences on Interpersonal Adaptation and Personality Development? In *Handbook of attachment: theory, research, and clinical applications*, eds. Jude Cassidy and Phillip R. Shaver, 198-225. New York: Guilford Press.

# Postscript

After over twenty years of marriage with no children, we became "surprise parents," if there is such a term. Frankly, we were not at all prepared for raising an animal, except for our short experience of adopting a stray kitten. During the pregnancy, we had many discussions about parenting. After looking at popular parenting books and hearing about many "common" approaches to parenting, we were not really satisfied. To us, the information was full of superficial and/or doubtful "how to's" (many of them seemed even harmful) but not much "principles." So, we asked the question: What would be the most important parenting principles?

After reading with open minds, we chose the following four themes as our core parenting principles: (1) child-parent attachment, (2) emotional development and self-regulation, (3) moral development, and (4) complex systems thinking and mindfulness. A few years passed; we had been busy with our daughter. Then, we started to think about how to celebrate our daughter's upcoming birthdays without materialistic practice. One of our answers was to write a children's book dedicated to our daughter. This time, for her third birthday, we wrote a story relevant to the first of our parenting principles focusing on attachment theory. But our story turned out as in Part 1. That is, it underscores attachment theory, but it is about making sense of one's life; it is neither from the children's perspective nor for parents to establish secure attachment with a child. Since the ideas underlying the story are fairly complex, both for children and adults, we changed our plan and adopted the current format, including a commentary. We look forward to reading the story to our daughter at some time, if not on or near her third birthday.

And we hope our daughter will read the commentary when she is old enough.

Another question we often ask is: What would be the best we can give to our daughter, if we die a few years later, a few moments later, or even right now? Our answer should be based on our core principles. For the first few years, we have been trying our best so that our daughter can be securely attached to us. This is for her to make sense of herself and also to overcome future, potential difficulties involving relationships. As our daughter approaches three years old, our focus is gradually shifting from attachment to other principles. For example, we try to make sure that at least one of us will be *available* to our daughter as she learns how to self-regulate and go through the basics of moral development. We wanted to do this even if we must sacrifice the possibility of saving for college or leaving her an inheritance. One of us even gave up an almost ideal job to support our plan.

As we proceed, we realize that the process of pursuing our principles is not at all easy. Even though we understand the points made in the book, our practice tends to fall short. We know that the "approach" mindset, even for negative things/events, is good. We know that the important thing is our daughter's understanding of us, not our perception of her understanding. Nevertheless, we often stumble. We also carry legacy attachment issues with our parents as well, and they disturb us occasionally. We hope that our daughter has as little attachment issues as possible.

While we explore our core parenting principles, we also ponder more mundane topics, such as education and work. Our daughter motivates us to think and reflect. Through the interaction with her, we are also learning to see things in their own light, with as few assumptions as possible. By suspending assumptions involved in conventional thinking, we start to see things differently. For example, we view education mainly as a process of learning the virtue of complexity around us (e.g., in physical, biological, psychological, social domains), and not as a process of pursuing high test scores, good grades, degrees, and even superior subject knowledge and technical skills. We are also interested in how one could gain meaningful working experience, although this topic will not be relevant to our daughter for a while. When the time comes, we will write our experience.

In the story, we used hippos as our characters. This choice was not crucial; our daughter happens to like hippos, along with other animals. The story is a work of fiction. Names, characters, and incidents are the product of the authors' imagination, and any resemblance to actual hippos, wild or captive, or other real-world situations is purely coincidental.

# Acknowledgments

We would like to thank every moment of our lives. We would also like to thank all living and non-living forms present at each moment. Since the involved party is so huge, we decided not to list them, including the names of people we would normally acknowledge in a book like this.

To us, the fact that our bodies have been functioning more or less all right for over forty years is a miracle. To us, the fact that our daughter, Anna, was conceived and born is beyond our imagination. To us, the fact that we were able to share our joys and sorrows through emotional communication with our relatives and friends is incredible. To us, the fact that our town, country, and the global community somehow function while also struggling with their own existence is an example of irreducible complexity. To us, the fact that all the forms in the universe somehow appear, transform, and disappear is an eternal mystery.

All of these create meaning in our lives. We are grateful to them.

# Index

incomplete sentences (in
 narratives), 56
inconsistent narrative, 56, 63
independence, 3, 4, 42, 47, 49, 73,
 84, 92
indirect path (relationship-
 meaning connection), 87
infantile amnesia, 56, 69
innate desire, 40
insecure, 76
insecure (attachment patterns), 47,
 52, 53, 54, 59, 68, 71, 72, 73,
 75, 77, 80, 88, 89, 93, 95, 97
 niche of, 48
intention, 87, 97
interaction, non-facial, 59
internal working model, 42, 60, 85,
 87
intimacy, 42, 47, 92
intrusiveness, 45, 46, 70, 74
Israel, 49
IWM. *See* internal working model

## J

joy, 66

## K

Kagan, J., 94
Karen, R., 37, 75, 92–97
Karr-Morse, R., 92
Kazui, M., 95, 96
Kennell, J., 96
Kibbutz, 49, 93
Kisii, 58, 59, 94
Klaus, M., 96
Kobak, R., 94
Kohn, A., 81, 95, 96
Kübler-Ross, E., 97

## L

left hemisphere, 66, 91, 95, *see also*
 right-left hemispheric
 integration

left-right. *See* right-left
 hemispheric integration
leniency, 79
Leo, P., 95
Lewis, M., 94
Lieberman, A., 95
life history theory, 95
limbic system, 61, 62, 65, 85
Little Match Girl, The, 89
love, substitute for, 73

## M

Main, M., 53, 95
making sense. *See* meaning
marriage, 7, 14, 77
maternal deprivation, 41, 70, 77,
 87
Maxims of Conversation, 54, 57
meaning, 22, 34, 36, 38, 39, 51, 65,
 67, 68, 77, 79, 80, 83, 84, 85,
 86, 87, 88, 92
measurement. *See* attachment
 measurement
medication, 47
meditation. *See* mindfulness
 meditation
memory, 18, 37, 39, 43, 60, 61, 62,
 65, 67, 69, 70, 92, *see also*
 implicit memory, explicit
 memory, semantic memory,
 autobiographical memory
mental representation, 60, 94
Mercer, J., 96
mindfulness, 87, 91, 97, 103
mindfulness meditation, 87, 97
mirror neurons, 97
mirror test, 67
monkey, 64, 94
moral development, 81, 91, 96,
 103, 104
motivation
 extrinsic vs. intrinsic, 88
 for caring, 74
mourning, 64, 94
Munholland, K., 96